PLACES

The "Our Alberta Heritage" Series

By Jacques Hamilton

Illustrated by Tom Nelson

COMMISSIONED BY CALGARY POWER LTD.

CALGARY, ALBERTA, CANADA

Printed in Canada

INTRODUCTION

The landscape that eventually became Alberta has remained substantially unchanged since the Ice Age. It took the pioneers of this province to turn landscape to landmark. As we examine the PLACES in Alberta's history we find that the early settlers selected homesteads, based upon the necessities of life. Did the new homestead provide for adequate shelter, food and livelihood? Were there friendly neighbors? Was there a water supply?

At locations where these requirements were filled, settlements sprang up, forts were erected, ranches developed, claims staked and townships grew.

Some of the stories of living conditions are heart-breaking, others have rewarding endings, but all have the same underlying message: the early pioneers to Alberta were seeking, and in most cases found, a new life for themselves and their families.

This volume, utilizing a few stories, unfolds the spirit of the early pioneer and his search for survival in a new environment.

— G. H. Thompson
Chairman of the Board
Calgary Power Ltd.

It is impossible to name them all here, but we would like to express our gratitude to the hundreds of Albertans who so graciously gave their time, their help and their rare records to make this project possible. There are two other people we would like to thank particularly: Mrs. Edith Smith of Calgary and Mrs. Naomi Radford of Edmonton. Without their efforts, these books could never have been completed.

— J. H.

CONTENTS

For Condensed Bibliography see end of People book

THE LEGEND

"NOT THE END, BUT THE BEGINNING!" . . .

It was 1650, a winter of bitter cold and famine, and inside a lodge of the mountain tribes the two greatest medicine men of the Rocky Mountains were in bitter contest.

Beeny and Gustlee had each had a vision, a vision of white-skinned people. To Gustlee, on one side of the smoking lodge fire, these white-skins were the Kannawdzets — vicious dwarfs who would tear the tribes of the mountain limb from limb.

To Beeny, they were the Sky People, and they would bring with them peace and prosperity.

"Our lives shall be a blessing," Beeny shouted over the taunts of his opponent. "Hard work shall be unnecessary, food shall always be plentiful."

Gustlee scoffed and the wise men of the mountain tribes, sitting to either side of the medicine men, swayed with Gustlee's scorn. But Beeny was not to be silenced.

"In my dream I saw the things which are slowly moving towards our country: the dogs of the sky (horses) that will come across the flatlands and over the mountain passes.

Though large as moose, they are gentle, docile; the horn of their feet is not cloven, but all one.

"They drag loads after them, and live among the people as our dogs do.

"I saw the goats of the sky (cattle) living in herds near the villages, whose flesh is used in the place of salmon.

"I saw strange people walking on earth, people almost like ourselves, whose bodies are covered with tight-fitting clothes, whose faces and hands are white like those of ghosts, and whose power is as great as that of manitous. I saw . . ."

Gustlee broke in. "Those strange beings are the Kannawdzets, the Kannawdzets I have seen at the mountain tops, the dwarfs that cause death whenever they are seen!"

Beeny ignored the interruption and went on:

"The white Sky-people I have seen in my dream will soon be coming to our country. The time is at hand when they will make life easy for us.

"They will show us how to cook in solid pots, without boiling boxes, thongs and red hot stones that burn our hands.

"Their axes cut the trees in four blows, their long sticks (guns) cast thunderbolts and kill the game a long way off.

"Their houses, two stories high, are warm in the winter, and the fire always stays invisible within a black box (stove) in the centre.

"They sow in the ground outside seeds that grow into plants, and the plants feed them when the cold moons return.

"The people, the ghost-like people are coming, I tell you, my friends! And those shall be the good days that change our lives and our ways, the days that Zazeekry is bringing from the eastern sky-land to the land of our forefathers . . ."

Gustlee, arms folded, stood grimly shaking his head. "Those ghost-like beings," he argued, "are nothing but the Kannawdzets I have seen up the crags. Beware, my friends! They can do no good, they mean only harm, death. If they come to us, the end is near."

"No! No!" screamed Beeny, eyes glazed with his vision. "Not the end, but the beginning!"

Neither man emerged from the medicine lodge that night the victor. And the wise men, shivering back to their own lodges, shook their heads in confusion at the words of the medicine man Beeny.

It was, after all, a curious vision for the 1650's. Especially for isolated mountain Indians who knew nothing of the Europeans gathering at the eastern end of the Great Lakes; Europeans for whom the Canadian west was still an un-drawn map.

What was it Beeny had said? "Not the end, but the beginning . . ."

TRADING POSTS

With all our modern pre-occupation with oil and cattle and grain, it's easy to forget what really started the move to settlement of Alberta — a soggy, rather dumb little animal with protruding yellow teeth and a furry hide. Castor Canadensis; the beaver.

Until the 1700's, the Alberta beaver led a tranquil existence. It was a simple round of building a dam here and a lodge there, and mooring a few choice young willow and aspen branches in the mud for winter snacks.

The only human threat was that of the occasional Indian hunter who had the unfriendly idea of converting the beaver's coat into a coat of his own. It was an idea the beaver did his best to discourage.

In 1690, a man named Henry Kelsey followed his curiosity west. The visit, the first to Alberta by a white man, didn't make much of a stir in beaver circles.

But a hundred years later that visit was going to have the beavers fighting — literally — for their skins.

What excitement was generated by Kelsey's reports of

his western explorations — including the report of the presence of beaver — was short-lived.

Game in what is now Ontario and Quebec provided more than enough fur to meet the demands of the time. And people were still too busy trying to "civilize" the east to think seriously of doing the same thing for the west.

But, as the 1700's moved on, feelings changed. The east was getting crowded and — much more importantly — something was happening on the European fashion scene.

Ever the dictator, fashion had decreed that no English gentleman was complete unless properly topped by a beaver hat.

English gentlemen, being no slouches in the fashion department, immediately set up a loud and passionate cry for beaver toppers.

Being good businessmen they also set up the machinery to make sure that what went on their heads did something to fatten their purses as well. The great fur game was on.

Dueling their way across the continent, the Hudson's Bay men and the Nor'westers stitched the northern prairies together with trading forts. In Alberta alone, 42 forts went up between 1778 and 1864.

Then, stung by the impudence of John Jacob Astor who was coolly creating an American fur monopoly on the coast of British Columbia, the Bay men and Nor'westers pushed on to break the barrier of the Rockies.

Those first trader-explorers — men like Peter Pond and David Thompson — were hardly settlers. (Unless "settling" in one spot long enough for a hurried meal or a few hours sleep qualify.)

No, it was those who followed — the sharp-penned and careful merchants who manned the posts — who really started settlement in Alberta.

Not that these "gentlemen-traders" were the mild-mannered merchants one sees today. Far from it. With Hudson's Bay and Northwest posts usually set up in sight of one another (and once or twice inside the same stockade) so that each side could keep track of the competition, the early traders had to be wily and tough and ready for anything.

Indeed, it was to be expected that when a post was doing too much better than the competition, chances of a sudden fire of "mysterious" origin became astronomically high.

The competition was guaranteed to show up a little too late with an offer of help. And to cluck sympathetically over the ashes. And, far from incidentally, to remind Indian customers that business was going on as usual across the street.

Fire sales weren't quite the same thing in the 1700's as they are today.

Indian customers, of course, were stirred to great heights

of activity by the sudden interest in fur. For enough fur —
preferably beaver pelts — an Indian could get virtually anything he wanted: knives and hatchet-heads and blankets and
colored cloth and ribbons and beads. Even tobacco and tea.

And the bargains! Why, all an Indian had to do to buy
a Hudson's Bay rifle, for example, was match its height in
beaver pelts.

So enthused were the Indian customers by bargains like
these that sometimes the same customer would show up two
or three days in a row — equipped every time with a pile of
pelts that bore a curious resemblance to some that had disap-
peared from the post the night before.

All the trading clerk could do under the circumstances
would be to offer a dry compliment on the trapper's ability.
And all the Indian could do would be to shrug modestly —
and wonder how soon the supply of padlocks would arrive
from the east.

And all the beaver —who started the whole thing —
could do was huddle in his lodge and hope fervently that
the spotlight of fashion would shift from him to buffalo
coats or something . . .

* * * *

MEANWHILE, DOWN AT THE BORDER . . .

It was the summer of 1874 and Rev. John McDougall, a
missionary at Morley, was on his way to pay a social call —
to the notorious whiskey fort, Fort Whoop-up.

"Crossing the Belly River," he wrote later for posterity,
"we rode up to the fort. We found the gate shut and very
little sign of humanity around. But presently the gate opened to us and we entered.

"Joseph Healy was in charge and had but one man with

him, for at the time the others were away interviewing members of the Boundary Commission, which was now about finishing the work of survey to the foot of the Rockies. Both countries interested had troops of soldiers and engineers working together determining the 49th parallel from Red River to the mountains. These had been at work since 1872.

"Healy told us he expected the Whoop-up contingent back any minute and asked us to make ourselves welcome in the fort and, as his man was more or less under the influence and he himself pretty well braced, he set to work preparing a meal for our party.

" 'Unbuckle and lay off your armoury for the moment, Parson John,' was his kind injunction to myself, and while we were at lunch he discussed the situation from his standpoint.

"There was not much need for government intervention in this country. He and his friends had been able to and kept the rougher element out.

"For instance, there was So-and-so. He came in and was going to run things. He lies under the sod at Standoff. And there was So-and-so. He had aspirations and we stretched him beside the first. And there was So-and-so. He went wild and we laid him out at Freezeout. And some more at Slideout.

"These bad men could not live in this country. We simply could not allow it. 'No, Parson John, we did not let any really bad men stay in this Whoop-up region' . . ."

A visitor to Lethbridge today — if he's hardy enough — can wade through some rapids to the remains of a shallow well and a battered cairn that mark the spot where the conversation recorded by 'Parson John' took place.

Or he can drive to a historic site south of the city and trace the deep ruts cut a century ago by the bull-trains that led to Whoop-up from Fort Benton in Montana.

Or he can do what thousands of others have done and visit the excellent replica of Whoop-up the Kinsmen have erected in Lethbridge's Indian Battle Park.

Whichever place he chooses, if he spends a few minutes considering Joe Healy's fervent reassurance that "we did not let any really bad men stay in this Whoop-up region," the visitor will have to conclude that old Joe wasn't a strictly truthful man.

Because, for the most part, the American free-traders who created Whoop-up and Standoff and the other whiskey posts were indeed "bad" men.

With few exceptions, they were outlaws who cheated, stole, and murdered. Some of their excesses outraged a whole country and one — the so-called "Cypress Hills massacre" — was the main reason for the birth of the North-West Mounted Police.

But, ironically, it is these same "bad" men who have to be given most of the credit for opening southern Alberta to settlement.

By 1869, decades of fur-trading activity had given a start to the settlement of northern Alberta. Posts like Fort Edmonton and Rocky Mountain House were gradually becoming the centres of small villages.

But south of the fur posts, Alberta was still largely a grassy and silent wilderness. It would take the whoops of the whiskey men to break the silence.

* * * *

OHHHH, GIVE ME A HOME . . .

It was December, 1869, in Montana Territory, and two free-traders were brooding over the injustices of federal government. So upset were Joe Healy and A.B. Hamilton that they were drowning their grief in their own whiskey — a sure sign that things must have been very bad indeed.

"Things," Healy ventured bitterly, "are just gettin' too civilized around here." Hamilton nodded sad agreement. It was all too true.

Fort Benton was turning into a regular town. Women were talking about Paris hats and men about ranching and it was getting so a man couldn't sleep for train whistles and church bells.

Worse than that, government control had arrived — with federal marshals and federal troops to enforce it. Which, for free-traders like Hamilton and Healy, meant an end to ignoring the silly law that said you couldn't trade whiskey to Indians.

Indeed, some of those federal marshals weren't above shooting a trader who was doing no more than help an Indian customer to a friendly drink or two. Montana, definitely, was getting to be an unhealthy place to do business.

Beyond the Canadian border, on the other hand . . . Hamilton and Healy were suddenly struck by an idea and they stared at one another. Then they leaned back and started to laugh and laugh and laugh.

* * * *

"LET'S WHOOP UP" . . .

Fort Whoop-up, at the junction of the St. Mary's and Belly river (now the Oldman River) started out in 1869 under the respectable name of Fort Hamilton. When the first crude fort burned down in the spring of 1870, its replacement was again named Fort Hamilton. How the name was changed has been the subject of many stories; all contradictory.

The most popular story of the origin of the name is that

a man who had returned to Fort Benton told people there that they were "really whoopin' it up" at Hamilton and Healy's post.

The most likely explanation is the one that was offered in The Lethbridge Herald in 1912:

The naming of Fort Whoop-up is traceable to a Frenchman named Charles Choquette, who freighted from Fort Benton to what was then Fort Hamilton. Choquette did not know much English, and whenever he learned a word he had a habit of repeating it over and over. There was an eighty-mile barren stretch between Fort Benton and Fort Hamilton, and it was a dread to the outfits that made the trip. One night Choquette was drawing near to the fort; his outfit was tired and lagging, and the others were complaining, including Charlie. Finally, someone said: "Let's whoop up and get to the fort." This struck Charlie as a good phrase, and he kept repeating it now and then. As they neared the fort he yelled "Whoop Up", and it became a byword.

* * * *

How the second-most famous whiskey fort, Fort Standoff, got its name is no mystery at all.

It earned the name for the biggest bluff in Alberta history.

Hard on the heels of Hamilton and Healy came dozens of other Montana free-traders, among them two men named Joe Kipp and Charlie Thomas.

The pair, however, faced a tougher escape from the United States than did the Whoop-up duo. It was now 1870, and Montana had a marshal whose name was Hard and whose reputation was harder still.

Marshal Hard was determined to keep Montana dry. He'd already confiscated several stocks of liquor at Fort Benton.

And he'd warned the free-traders that any wet goods found in the Indian territory — which included Benton and several hundred miles of country around it — would be seized.

Kipp and Thomas knew the marshal meant business, but they also figured that they had a scheme to outwit him.

They'd simply go outside Indian territory and buy a large quantity of liquor and race it across the line into Canada — cutting off the Blackfoot trade that had been going to Benton.

Kipp headed for Helena, Montana, to start the plan rolling. But, riding right behind, was the ever-suspicious Marshal Hard.

Kipp knew the marshal was behind him. In Helena, he managed to dodge his follower long enough to buy 75 cases of high-proof liquor and arranged to have it delivered, secretly, to a spot on the Missouri River just below the town.

There Kipp hurriedly built a raft, loaded the cases aboard, and floated off to the mouth of the Sun River (the present site of Great Falls).

Waiting for him was Thomas with three four-horse teams and a hired man.

Knowing that the persistent marshal couldn't be too far behind, they threw cases onto the wagons and took off, heading straight north to the Canadian border as fast as they could travel.

Three days later, just after fording a river, Kipp looked back and saw a lone rider hot in pursuit.

Kipp didn't have to guess who it was.

"It's the marshal," he muttered to his partner, "and right here is where we stand him off."

The triumphant marshal reined in and ordered Kipp to turn his outfit around and head back to Benton.

"Turn back?" Kipp was wounded. He shook his head. Then, slowly, a grin spread over his face and he leaned back.

"You know, marshal, you're just 20 minutes too late. We cross the boundary line at the North Fort back there."

The marshal exploded. He ranted. He raved. He threatened.

Kipp grinned. He yawned. He scratched his chin. He winked at Charlie Thomas.

Finally Marshal Hard stopped for breath — and to think the situation over. Kipp might be right. At least, he certainly seemed to think he was. And then there was the matter of three guns to one.

Hard took one last, regretful look at the wagons and their gurgling loads. Then he wheeled his horse with a curse and headed back to Benton.

Kipp never forgot the encounter. When he and Thomas built their fort on the Belly River, they named it after the confrontation.

Kipp re-told the story hundreds of times, but never with quite as much delight as he did right after the International Boundary Commission, turned in its report in 1874.

It seems that when the marshal caught up with them, Kipp and company were still 300 yards within the confines of the good old U.S. of A.

* * * *

"WE HAD A FEW GOOD YEARS" . . .

The era of the free-traders in southern Alberta lasted a short five years. And the first few of those years were a lot more peaceful than many would like us to believe.

The real failure of the whiskey forts was their success.

Kipp and the Standoff crowd had figured to cut off the trade to Benton. They succeeded admirably. During their first spring, they were able to ship south more than 3,000 prime buffalo robes and 2,000 small furs while Benton went bare. And other traders were doing just as well or, in the case of Fort Whoop-up, even better.

But what the free-traders didn't realize was that they were having even more of an effect on the fur-trade to the north.

Before the invasion of the free-traders, the merger of the Nor'westers and Hudson's Bay Company had created an enormous fur monopoly. The Whoop-up crowd had broken the monopoly, and the Hudson's Bay Company wasn't going to let them get away with it.

Almost from the moment the free-traders crossed the border, Ottawa was subjected to a barrage of complaints and exaggerated reports — virtually all from the Hudson's Bay Company, or inspired by them.

By 1871, these reports were taking on a serious tone:

"Indians visiting the Rocky Mountain House during the fall of 1870 have spoken of the existence of a trading post of Americans from Fort Benton, upon the Belly River, sixty miles within the British boundary-line. They have asserted that two American traders, well-known on the Missouri, named Culvertson and Healy, have established themselves at this post for the purpose of trading alcohol, whiskey, and arms and ammunition of the most improved description, with the Blackfeet Indians; and that an active trade is being carried on in all these articles, which, it is said, are constantly smuggled across the boundary-line by people from Fort Benton."

The next year, Col. Robertson-Ross, head of the Canadian Militia, submitted an even more ominous report:

"Beyond the Province of Manitoba westward, there is no kind of government at all, and no security of life and property beyond what people can do for themselves. Serious crimes have been allowed to go unpunished . . .

"When at Rocky Mountain House I was informed that a party of American smugglers and traders had established a trading post at the junction of the Bow and Belly Rivers, about 30 miles due east of the Porcupine Hills and 60 miles on the Dominion side of the boundary. This trading post they have named Fort Hamilton, after the mercantile firm of Hamilton, Healy and Company, of Fort Benton, Montana, from whom they obtain their supplies. It is believed that they number about 20 men, under command of John Healy, a notorious character . . .

"It is stated on good authority that, in 1871, 88 of the Blackfeet were murdered in drunken brawls."

It's significant that both reports originated from Rocky Mountain House — a Hudson's Bay post.

These reports, however, were being supported by others of unquestionable sincerity — from the missionaries working among the Indians.

"Since last autumn," lamented Father Lacombe, "the process of demoralization has, alas!, made very considerable progress; the disorders of all kinds which have taken place among the savages and these miserable traders of rum are frightful.

"We have done our best to inform the American Government of these unhappy infringements of its laws; while on the other side the government of the Red River has made a very severe law prohibiting intoxicating liquors throughout these territories.

"But while we await the coming of some impressive force to compel the fulfilment of this wise law, we suffer unceasingly."

The combined pressure of military, church, and the biggest mercantile empire in Canada couldn't be ignored in Ottawa. Soon the government was stirring into action.

If the free-traders hadn't been aware of the Hudson's Bay Company when they crossed the border, rumors of the reports to Ottawa had them conscious of them now. And the Bay men were threatening to make the presence felt in a more direct way as well.

When Hamilton and Healy rebuilt Fort Whoop-up in the spring of 1870, they spent $20,000 turning it into an armed fortress. Modelled on Fort Benton, Whoop-up bristled with cannon and was fully stocked with grape and cannister shot.

They took all this trouble not because of hostile Indians, but because of threatened attack by the Hudson's Bay Company.

Hamilton and Healy may have wondered, uneasily, why their powerful enemies never bothered following up the threat.

Unknown to the free-traders, their posts — particularly Whoop-up — were creating scandal on both sides of the border. The public was turning strongly against the practice of trading rot-gut liquor to Indians. And the American newspapers were having a field-day painting pictures of horror at the border posts.

Years later, Fred Kanouse, a veteran of the Whoop-up era, could see all too clearly what none of the free-traders had been able to see at the time.

"The source of Whoop-up's reputation as a rendezvous of bad men," he told an interviewer, "is traceable to a San Diego, California, newspaper. The story must have been more than a column, and was about as lurid as imagination could make it.

"It is said that Fort Whoop-up was the rendezvous of the bloodiest band of cut-throats that ever went unhung, including escaped convicts, murderers, renegades, and that ilk, who pillaged and murdered Indians, stole horses and cattle, and did many other things equally as bad.

"It is true that there were such men along the border at that time. But they were not a part of those who made the fort their headquarters.

"At no time were there more than sixty men at the post, and in most cases five or six traders was all that remained when the trappers and wolfers were out seeking pelts.

"In those days it was policy to be on good terms with

the Indians, as we traders were doing a good business and desired that friendly relations remained unbroken . . .

"There were stirring times along the border about that time, and many men who were not willing to have their past investigated, but contrary to popular belief, Fort Whoop-up was not the gathering place for them, but the home of traders and trappers."

Kanouse, of course, was inclined to lean a little to the generous side in his recollections.

* * * *

IS THERE A DOCTOR IN THE HOUSE? . . .

Perhaps the fairest description of the men of the whiskey forts came from the pen of Morley missionary Rev. John McDougall, who was trusted and respected by virtually all of them.

At one point, Rev. McDougall was paid a visit by the Rev. Laughlin Taylor, general secretary of the Methodist Church. When it came time for Dr. Taylor to leave, McDougall decided to take him home via Fort Benton.

The first stop was Fort Kipp, one of the smaller whiskey posts, where the party picked up some tinned fruit (which Rev. McDougall had never seen before) and an escort of drunken, boisterous free-traders.

Dr. Taylor, who had previously visited the Holy Land, did his best to offset the effect of the escort by lecturing the whiskey men on "The Land of the Bible."

McDougall prudently doesn't record the audience's reaction to the lecture.

"On to Whoop-up," his chronicle states. "Across the Belly at Fort Kipp, and up the big hill, and out across the wide upland, and with our wild, uproarious, heavily armed escort whooping and yelling and cursing, we drove and rode and wondered what might come next.

"Presently we looked down upon the junction of the St. Mary's and Belly Rivers, two deep valleys, quite well timbered with fine bottom lands of prairie intersecting . . . Here was the fort, strongly built of cottonwood and poplar logs, and further down was another post . . ."

McDougall and Dr. Taylor spent a few pleasant hours at Whoop-up, chatting with friends of the Morley missionary. Then, rid finally of their Kipp escort, they headed towards Fort Benton.

On the east bank of the St. Mary's River, they decided to stop and eat their tinned fruit. Just as they'd begun, they heard a terrific racket coming from the west.

McDougall writes: "Around the woods came a troop of horsemen, a wilder, swearing, whooping lot seldom could be seen. They were after us for some reason, that was plain, and they were evidently wild with whiskey. Right into the river they plunged, and never let up until they had surrounded our party.

"It had come to pass that almost immediately after we left Fort Whoop-up a party had come in from the northeast. These had been fighting with the Indians, and one man was brought in all 'shot up'.

"Then the rumor had gone out that a doctor had just passed through; so this party gathered up to come after the doctor.

"We had a time explaining to them the difference between medicine and divinity . . ."

* * * *

THE GREEN RIVER RENEGADE

Had the free-traders been alone in coming to Alberta, they

might have hung on in the border country a little longer. But they weren't alone.

Trailing behind, and soon outnumbering them, were the wolfers.

Not satisfied to rely on rifles to hunt, they coldly poisoned game across the plains.

These wolfers were the real-life counterparts of the rumoured "murderers in the south." Most of them thought nothing of killing a man who crossed them. Human life was absolutely without value. And they considered the Indian even less than human.

It was one of these wolfers, Thomas Hardwick, known as the Green River Renegade, who finally brought the Whoop-up era to an end.

In 1873, Hardwick was 29 and the acknowledged leader of the Alberta-Montana wolfers.

Born in Missouri, he'd served in the Confederate Army, and traded among the Indians in Wyoming during 1869 and 1870.

At some point in his life, he'd acquired a fanatic hatred for Indians and, while in Wyoming, he was captured twice by tribes bent on punishing him. He managed to escape each time.

Moving to Montana, he was involved in several fights with Indians. In February, 1871, he is known to have murdered one Crow Indian and wounded another.

The next spring, he was wolfing in the Sweetgrass Hills of Alberta; setting out poisoned buffalo carcasses to kill the wolves. His party had already had one or two run-ins with Peigan Indians, and shortly after sunrise on April 5, 1872, Hardwick spotted a party of Indians on a nearby hill.

The Indians were Assiniboines, but Hardwick took them for Peigans or Bloods. Without warning, he opened fire.

In the fight that followed, four Indians were killed and ten others wounded.

Then, in May, 1873, Hardwick was leading a group of wolfers back to Fort Benton from a successful winter on the plains around Calgary.

Cree Indians ran off their horses near Benton. Hardwick's party rushed into Benton, grabbed new horses, and set off in pursuit.

Days later, on Battle River in the Cypress Hills, the trackers located a camp of Assiniboines. The Indians weren't the horse thieves, but the enraged Hardwick — again without warning — opened fire. The rest of his party followed suit.

Minutes later, between 30 and 80 Indians — men, women and children — lay dead.

News of the massacre reached Ottawa in a matter of days — exaggerated to the point where parliament was told that "more than 200" Indians had been brutally slaughtered.

Ottawa, already goaded by three years of increasingly disturbing reports from the west, acted immediately. On May 23, 1873, only three weeks after Hardwick opened fire, the North-West Mounted Police force was created, with orders to tame the west and drive out the whiskey traders.

Late the next year, Col. James F. Macleod led his red-coated force up to the gates of Fort Whoop-up.

But news of his arrival had travelled ahead of him. Most of the wolfers and traders had fled back to the U.S. (Hardwick, for example, was never punished, and ended his days in 1901 as a prosperous businessman in Missouri.)

The gates of Fort Whoop-up were opened by Dave Akers, the only one of the traders to remain behind. Friendly in the extreme, he showed the colonel his vegetable garden (but not the whiskey kegs buried under it), and communicated

Healy's offer to sell the fort to the mounties for $25,000.

Col. Macleod rejected the offer as too high. Then he ordered his men to tear down the free-trader flag over Whoop-up, and had them raise the Union Jack.

With its raising, the Whoop-up era came to an end.

And, today, standing between the well and battered cairn, the visitor can almost hear the earnest assurance of Joe Healy that:

"No, Parson John, we did not let any really bad men stay in this Whoop-up region . . ."

PIONEER HARDSHIPS

AN END TO SILENCE . . .

No one can say honestly that he knows why they came. But they came.

Perhaps it was the lure of the legendary Chinooks or tales of grassy plains that had never known a plough. Or perhaps it was just the dream of a frontier.

They pushed north from Montana behind bawling herds of cattle, or west from Winnipeg in wagons loaded with household effects and brave women and crying children.

And even when the Chinooks proved only rare respites from the bitterness of winter, and even when their ploughs turned nothing but dust, they stayed on.

It was a desperate fight, but slowly — furrow by furrow — they won it. Sometimes the price of winning was bitter. In every churchyard in Alberta there are graveplots, some only two feet long, that count the cost they paid.

And on headstone after headstone is carved the one-word epitaph that is the proudest any Albertan can earn: "Pioneer."

* * * *

The Whoop-up era was dead, but as the last three decades

of the 19th century spun away it was obvious that what had started with Whoop-up wasn't going to end with it.

In 1870, a young American named Nicholas Sheran had come through Whoop-up on his way to search for gold. Instead of gold, however, he found coal, and by 1874 he was busy chipping away at exposed seams on the Belly River — and unknowingly digging the foundations of Lethbridge.

The North-West Mounted Police, having torn down the Whoop-up flag, were now 30 miles west; building Fort Macleod and the core of what would be Alberta's first true "town."

In the open space between the fur posts and whiskey forts, wagon ruts were beginning to replace the snaking trails of Indian travois.

At Red Deer Crossing, four young bachelors had already raised a few crude log huts and new arrivals, many of them families, were beginning to build near them.

Legitimate trading companies, like the I.G. Baker Co., moved in to take the place of the whiskey traders. On their heels came smaller traders, often one-man operations, to fan out and give budding settlements their first "stores."

In Fort Benton, Montana, in 1877, readers of the fort's newspaper, The River Press, noted with interest a small announcement:

"Joseph McFarlane and Miss Marcella Sheran were married at Fort Whoop-up, N.W.T., on the fourth of July last. Father Scollen performed the ceremony and the happy couple received the salute of six guns from Fort Whoop-up. After the ceremony, they were escorted to the McFarlane home by their friends. This is the first marriage of a white couple recorded at Whoop-up. Such is the progress of civilization."

THE BREATH OF OUR BEAUTIFUL CHINOOK . . .

Many Alberta pioneers, right into the 20th Century, were brought here, literally, by the wind.

If Alberta has a magic word, it's "Chinook"; the word for a west wind that sweeps down from the Rockies, raising temperatures as much as 45 degrees in 12 hours and melting a foot of snow and ice at a time.

Indian legend has it that Chinook was a beautiful maiden who wandered into the mountains of the southwest and was lost. For days and weeks, warriors searched for her without success.

Then, one day, a soft and warm breeze blew from the west. The elders of the tribe nodded their heads wisely. "It is the breath of our beautiful Chinook," they said, and the warriors searched no more.

The legends Alberta's early pioneers created weren't as beautiful, but they definitely rated higher in entertainment value.

There was hardly a prospective settler who hadn't heard of the man who'd driven his team into town in a blinding blizzard and hitched it to a pole — only to wake up the next morning in a Chinook and discover his team hanging from the top of the church steeple.

And the insistent claim of the trapper who said he'd raced ahead of a Chinook with his lead dog lost in driving snow and the runners of his sleigh kicking up a cloud of dust.

Lost alongside these tall tales was another Indian warning; one that held an ominous message no one heeded.

When winter passed without a warm wind, snow stayed and food supplies could not be replenished, and people died.

The Indians had a word for that death: a word that meant "no-wind."

* * * *

A LIGHT IN THE WINDOW . . .

Perhaps no story illustrates the meaning of the word better than that of Lee Brainard; a man who ended his days equating the word "Chinook" with the worst curses that man has devised.

Although the story took place in 1906, it is a vivid example of what happened to so many earlier pioneers who followed the wind and ignored good advice when they came to Alberta . . .

Lee Brainard was 47 years old, a widower with a teen-aged son, and a successful rancher in Montana. But he was tired of the work of gathering winter feed, and tired of ranching on over-crowded, over-grazed range.

Often, from wandering cowboys, he'd heard stories of the legendary Chinook belt where cattle could graze freely all year round.

It was, he'd been told, a country where a man with a stake could carve himself out a cattle empire.

The stories were attractive — and persistent — and Brainard finally decided to follow them to Alberta.

It was mid-summer when he, his son Albert, and an old hired hand named White set out. They had two covered wagons and a herd of 700 head of cattle; 450 yearlings and adults plus calves. They also had more than 100 horses.

With the occasional help of hired riders, they drove the herd northwest and across the Canadian border. Skirting the western fringe of the Cypress Hills, they pushed on to the valley of the South Saskatchewan and the young town of Medicine Hat.

In Medicine Hat, restocking supplies, Brainard came to the attention of the Mounted Police who heard of his plan to go into new country at the end of the summer with no feed supplies and no buildings put up for shelter.

The police were on the point of prohibiting him from going on, but decided instead to let him go with warnings of the dangers that lay ahead.

Brainard chose to ignore the warnings, and headed for the government land office.

There, to his disappointment, he found that all possible sites for a large spread along the South Saskatchewan, the Bow and the Red Deer rivers were already taken.

Brainard perked up, however, when the helpful agent pointed out that there was still a large expanse of land north of Red Deer with only a few scattered claims marked on it.

What the agent didn't tell Brainard, possibly because he assumed he already knew, was that the northern land was outside the Chinook belt.

Ignorant of the danger, Brainard, Albert and White restocked the wagons, rounded up the herd and headed north.

Days later, they forded the Red Deer and pushed up a large creek to a spot about three miles north of where the town of Richdale stands today.

Brainard thought he'd found the answer to his dreams: miles of open grassland, a creek for water and willows for shelter and fuel.

The trio lifted one of the wagon boxes from its chassis to serve as a home. Then they gathered a small supply of wood and chips for fuel, far too small a supply to meet the needs they had yet to learn existed.

Secure in the belief they were in the Chinook belt, Brainard's party spent most of their time exploring the new country around them.

On one of these rides, about 40 miles from camp, Brainard came upon the ranch of the Hunt brothers. The Hunts, finding out what position Brainard was in, urged him to bring all his calves and yearlings to them for wintering.

Brainard, being a stubborn man, refused.

One morning in mid-October, the Brainard party awoke with a shock to discover the ground covered with snow.

Brainard reasoned, however, that since it was still early in the year a Chinook was bound to come along and clear the snow away.

But there was no Chinook. Just snow and more snow.

Finally, the party moved its camp and the herd to hilly country near Dowling Lake where there was some shelter, and where the wind kept some of the ridges free of snow so the stock could get grass.

But with only the wagon for shelter, their plight was desperate. Week after week, the cold and storms continued. Christmas came and passed without a break.

January brought blizzards and temperatures that averaged 30 to 40 below zero.

Some of the cattle were already dying, and if it hadn't been for the horses pawing through to the grass, others would have perished.

Day after day, the three men grew weaker; huddling in the bitter cold of the wagon and eating nothing but skinny beef.

Brainard, tortured constantly by the cries of his dying cattle, bitterly regretted his stubbornness in ignoring the Mounties at Medicine Hat and in turning down the Hunts' offer to winter his stock.

His only hope was for a change in the weather; a break that would let him make a dash for the Hunts' and save part of the herd and their own lives.

On January 29, the break finally came in the form of a Chinook so warm the three were working in shirt sleeves before the day was out.

In a race against time, they gathered what cattle still had strength to move and shot the rest. They hitched Brainard's stallion and another horse to the covered wagon.

By dawn they were on their way, the rest of the horses being pushed ahead to break trail in the deep and soggy snow.

It was almost impossible going. They had to stop frequently to rest the lathered horses.

But, by noon, they had made a dozen miles. If the Chinook would hold another day, they'd make it to safety.

It was dead calm, and Albert and White made a small fire of willow twigs and roasted some fresh beef. They would eat and rest, then push on to the Hunts' ranch.

Suddenly, young Albert turned around and leapt to his feet. "For God's sake," he yelled. "Look what's coming!"

From the northwest, a towering grey wall of cloud was swirling down on them, kicking up writhing eddies of snow. In a moment the sun was blotted out.

Floundering through the snow, the three made a desperate attempt to catch their saddle horses, but all except Brainard's stallion got away as the storm struck.

They tried to take shelter in the wagon, but the wind tore through it in paralyzing blasts. It grew colder and colder until they could stand it no longer, and they had to get out and exercise to keep from freezing to death.

All night, with Brainard goading, the three marched round and round in a circle. Every so often they'd try to make a fire from willow twigs, but the flames would be torn away by the wind or buried in drifting snow.

By dawn, they were like statues of ice, floundering in a whirlpool of wind and snow. They could hardly breath and their legs were failing.

Finally, inevitably, the aged White stumbled. Young Albert grabbed him under the arms and yelled to his father. Before Brainard could reach the pair, White had gone limp and slipped from the boy's grasp to the ground.

Father and son worked feverishly over the man who had been their companion since Albert was born. But, long minutes later, they realized that White was dead.

With White dead, the boy seemed to lose all will to live. Brainard pummelled him with his fists, screamed, pleaded, but the boy wouldn't fight on. Finally, Brainard picked the boy up and struck out in the storm.

Even with all the strength of his fury, it was too much of an effort for Brainard. A bitter half-hour later he was back to lay the corpse of his son gently by that of his old friend's.

Brainard cut loose his stallion to give it a chance for survival. Then he explored the area around the wagon and found some of his cattle frozen upright in the snow.

Taking an axe from the wagon, he chopped pieces from them and ate the meat raw.

Then heading directly into the wind, he struggled towards the Hunts' ranch.

Hours later, delirious, he thought he saw the figure of a long dead friend walking towards him. He tried to pull off a mitt to shake the hand of the apparition before him, but the blast of the wind on his wrist snapped him back to sanity.

Still hours later, he bumped into something and collapsed in a faint.

But then he was conscious again, and realizing that what

he had fallen over was a fence.

No longer able to stand, he crawled alongside the wire on his hands and knees. He passed the feed corrals and came at last to the Hunt brothers' shack. He fell against the door.

Jack Hunt thought it was a steer at the door. "Get to hell out of there!" he yelled.

"I won't get out," was the weak response on the other side of the door and the startled Hunt brothers were immediately on their feet.

Dragging Brainard inside, the Hunts rubbed his frozen face, hands and feet with kerosene.

But the three brothers were virtually helpless. Brainard needed a hospital but the storm, distance, and his condition all conspired against moving him.

In the end, despite the efforts of the brothers, Brainard lost all but one of his toes. It took months for his face and hands to heal.

Brainard was eventually taken out to civilization and shipped to a hospital in Montana.

As soon as the storm eased, one of the Hunt brothers had gone out and covered the two bodies with snow to protect them from coyotes. So severe was the winter of 1906-7 that it was May before the Mounted Police could come out and move the bodies to Stettler.

Later the next summer, a partially recovered Brainard returned to try to find what was left of his herd. Of the 600 head he'd arrived with, he found only 15. Others of his animals, cattle and horses, continued to turn up — some in remote parts of Saskatchewan and Montana — for seven years afterwards.

Ruined and alone, Brainard went back to Montana to make a fresh start.

But he didn't go back to Montana to stay. Brainard still had the courage and determination that had carried him through the storm to Hunts' door. And he still had the dream that had brought him to Alberta in the first place.

Years later, remarried, he again headed north. This time he put wisdom to work and made it, living and ranching here until his peaceful death in 1938.

Lee Brainard was never known to talk of the storm that had cost him his only son and his old friend. But he had one eccentricity that proved the storm was never far from his thoughts.

To the end of his days he never allowed a blind drawn on any window in his home. He wanted his lights to shine out at all times as a guide to safety for anyone lost in darkness or a storm . . .

* * * *

THE GREAT TREK . . .

Even for the well-prepared, the trip to Alberta was filled with hardships. And no one could be better prepared than the 12 Mormon families who followed Charles Ora Card north to Canada in 1887.

They were no tenderfeet. They had pioneered once already, to carve out homesteads in Utah.

They knew the hardships of the trail, and they had no illusions about Chinooks or any other break that nature might offer.

In choosing to follow Charles Ora Card north, they knew they faced long weeks and months through dangerous country. And they knew that even when they reached Canada, it would take years to regain even the little comfort they had created in Utah.

Why did they come?

The reason is probably much simpler — and much more complicated — than religion alone can explain. Perhaps, as the words of a song written by one of those who made the trek suggests, it was simply that they were pioneers:

"I am just a pioneer —
Landed in the eighties here;
And the trail seemed long to Canada by team.
When I hear the coyote howl, and
The hooting of the owl,
Then I dream again my early manhood dreams . . ."

Card was a cautious man. Before proposing the trek north, he made a long trip of exploration and chose a spot by the side of Lee Creek, just south of the huge reserve left to the Blackfoot Indians by Treaty Number 7. On his way back to Utah, Card carefully mapped a route to that spot; mapped it so carefully that not one of the lonely wagons was lost for so much as a day.

In 1960, two of the last survivors of that trek, Jane Eliza Woolf Bates and Zina Alberta Woolf Hickman, wrote their memories of the famous trip:

"To us, the younger ones of the party, the coming trip was hailed as a challenging adventure. To our elders, who had been pioneers or the children of pioneers of Utah, it was a huge undertaking.

"They knew that the greater part of Idaho and Montana through which we were to travel was wild, Indian infested, unsettled country for the most part, with rugged mountains and turbulent rivers to cross. The roads were poor at the best, often cut through forests, and were sometimes only narrow trails.

"Our outfit, the Woolf's, consisted of father, mother, six children, two wagons and Henry Matkin, aged twelve, who helped drive the cattle and horses. There were thirty-six head of stock in the two outfits.

". . . We had two good teams of mares, other horses and cows and a white pony called Peter that all except the youngest child could ride when he was not otherwise on duty. One of our two wagons had a set of bed-springs fitted to an extension on the double-bed wagon box. This was for mother and the children.

"Aunt Zina's wagon was arranged the same way. All the wagons had two boxes and were well packed. These extension wagons carried prepared sandwiches and rusks in case it was necessary to satisfy our hunger while still driving to find camping places and water for the horses. They also carried changes of clothing, extra bedding and other emergency or needful commodities.

"Fastened on the back, outside of the two extension wagons were mother's rocking chair and Aunt Zina's camp chair. Our second wagon held bags of oats, flour, potatoes, and other vegetables, packed trunks of clothing, wooden wash tubs and wash board, and such things as hand plow, camp stove, shovel, axe, wrenches, wagon grease, pewter and tin table utensils, candle molds, bullet molds, nose bags for feeding oats to the horses, cooking pots and utensils, all of iron; tea-kettle, bake oven, frying pans; a rack made at one stop to accommodate a new-born calf which during the crossing of one very steep river had to be taken into the front of the wagon.

"Most of the towns we had looked forward to visiting were disappointingly small. I remember Camas, Swan Lake and Pocatello. The last was a small place which seemed to me to be surrounded by Indian encampments. I remember being impressed with the clean, bright appearance of the Indians, Bannocks, and of their surroundings. They seemed to be different and of a higher class than the Indians I had seen at home. We had no difficulty with them but kept careful watch over our stock.

"There were endless miles of sage brush, rough roads and often mud holes from which it took four and sometimes six horses to drag us.

"When Johnny was needed to assist others, or find fords, Mamie or I cared for young Joseph while his mother drove team and Sterling drove cattle.

"The cows sometimes became lame with cracked hoofs or with gravel in them. At such time two or three days' stop-over was necessary. The hooves were washed clean of gravel, filled with tar and wrapped with gunny sacking.

"During the layovers the women did the necessary baking and cooking, washing and mending. This also was the time when Aunt Zina and mother made as many light loaves of bread as was possible; and for bathing in the front of the wagons, with washtubs replacing the spring seats, and with covers drawn. . .

"Wagon wheels scretched and groaned and bumped along over long stretches of prairie when prairie dogs came out in numbers and barked at the intruders as we passed. A lone wolverine drank without fear from a stream that we crossed. There were many coyotes and badgers.

"From now on there were no roads, only old trails with ruts, stones, stumps and tree roots to keep us bumping. There were often stormy days with both snow and rain to add to the discomfort.

"It was often so cold the wagon covers had to be drawn tight and smooth over the bows and made close at the back. Often blankets were hung at the front, back of the driver, as well as at the back, to keep the cold and the driving rain and sleet out.

"What a happy relief when the sun shone and the front cover could be thrown back so we could feel the warmth! How pleasant to be able to see where we were and to look for something besides snow, mud and sage-brush! What an extreme joy we felt when we camped in the mountains where the steep slopes were covered with towering pines from which the boys brought us pine nuts!

"Weather permitting, we spent our evenings around the campfire. Sitting on spring-seats from the wagons, on packing boxes or fallen logs we listened to the sweet strains of the mouth organ played by Will Rigby and Brother John. One of the favorite songs of all was 'Hard Times Come Again No More', though often we sang hymns such as 'All is Well', and 'Oh Ye Mountains High, Where The Clear, Blue Sky Arches Over The Homes of The Free'. After prayers of praise and thanksgiving and petitions for continued guidance we retired to rest as best we might in cramped and crowded spaces.

"On reaching Helena it was found there was not enough water for bathing purposes so the children were bathed in skim milk.

"We made butter by tying the jar containing the cream to the back of the wagon. By night the jolting of the wagon had produced a nice pat of fresh butter, and the buttermilk made a refreshing drink. Carrying the milk had been a problem. At Helena mother purchased a tall tin dasher churn in which more butter at a time could be made. The milk was placed in covered pans and jars at night, the thick cream skimmed into the churn, and all the milk that could not be used or given away was thrown away. We could not permit the cows to go unmilked or they would dry up.

"There had been on our trip, no serious accidents, but two very close ones and in one mother was the victim.

"An axe in the hands of one of the young men chopping wood had flown off the handle and struck mother on the side of the head and she had fallen, fainting. The spot over her temple was very painful and she suffered from headaches. But she had good care and soon recovered.

"A horse kicked the Farrell driver, George Thompson, on the leg, but he too had good care and was soon able to take over his job again.

"The pioneers knew what to do in almost every case of accident or sickness, whether travelling or at home.

"Another near accident involved both mother and Wilford. While camped on Boulder Mountain a sudden dynamite blast from railroad workers sent a shower of rocks down the side. One huge boulder bounded down close to Wilford and just missed mother where she was dipping water from the stream. Camp was hastily moved to a safe distance.

"On the ninth of May, President Card and company,

travelling south, met the first advance company headed north for the new colony. By horse Brother Card travelled on to meet his family.

"Johnny, as usual driving the lead team, spotted the lone khaki clad rider approaching. The man alighted, tied his horse to a post of the wire fence along one side of the road and started for the wagon train.

"Johnny kept his eye on him, and as he stopped Aunt Zina's team, climbed in her wagon and kissed her, Johnny shouted to father who drove the team just behind him, 'Pa, that old galoot is getting in Aunt Zina's wagon ... He's kissing her!'

"Father had recognized his bewhiskered friend, C.O. Card, and gave the go-ahead sign and the wagon wheels rolled along.

"It was a joyful camp-making near Little Boulder Range that night. Brother Card recorded in his journal, 'It was a happy meeting to join my family and friends who had toiled through weeks of cold, stormy weather, over snow-capped mountains, hills and bleak plains. I found them in good spirits for they had leaned on the Lord.'

"The next morning, May 13th, we awoke to find six inches of snow on the ground and still snowing. There was poor food for the stock and no wood here, so we hitched up without breakfast and drove on about ten miles to within three-quarters of a mile of Little Boulder Mountain. Here we found plenty of water and snow-covered grass.

"However, the men borrowed a large tent from nearby railroaders, cleared away the snow, set it up, cut pine boughs to spread over the floor, spread horse blankets over them and made big fires without, and in the camp stoves within the big tent.

"The women cooked, the children played, the men talked with their leader and exchanged experiences. We ate together but slept in our wagons and were warm and comfortable. The next day the weather cleared and we drove on to the north side of Big Boulder Mountain . . .

"Occasionally we saw ahead of us a long mule or ox-team with several wagons drawn close together and an equal number of teams in front with the driver walking beside them cracking a long black whip over their backs. We never did get close enough to hear the language they used, though the ferocity of their voices left no doubt as to its meaning.

"From this point on near Choteau we had to start night-herding the horses. Brother Card took the first part of the night to 1 A.M. and father took the balance of the night. We were nearing Indian country and must be careful.

"We camped about six miles south of Dupuyer near a beautiful spring of water on May 27th, and on the 28th we camped on the north bank of Birch Creek on the Peigan

Reservation. Our wagons were growling in the congealed hub grease.

"On the next day we drove to the Indian agency to procure lumber to build a boat as the streams were swelling with the melting snow from the mountains. We waited for the stock and the men who helped to get them across Badget Creek, then drove to Medicine River which was very high.

"An Indian named Peter was engaged for the price of $2.50 to guide us to a safer crossing. About one and a half miles on, a place was found where the river had spread. Up-rooted trees and much debris had been carried down stream on the muddy waters. On examination it was found the approach to the river had been washed away and a new one must be dug out.

"While the new approach was being made ready, three Indian Police brought a note into camp written by the agent, Mr. W.D. Baldwin which read as follows:

May 29, 1887, To Whom It May Concern: A white or gray horse in your outfit is claimed as the property of one of the Indians belonging to the Agency. You will at once return to the Agency and account for same. The bearer is one of our Indian Police, the Captain of the force. Very truly, W.D. Baldwin.

"Peter, our white horse which we had brought from Hyde Park with us, was the horse in question.

"Henry Matkin had been riding him as he drove the cattle when the Indian claimed him. Henry refused to give the horse up or even to dismount, so the Indian had led him into camp by the bridle. Father, accompanied by his friend Brother Farrell, returned to the agency at Dupuyer and during the examination by the agent, the Indian was asked if there were any identifying marks by which he could prove his ownership.

"The Indian pointed to black spots on the pony's legs and another Indian swore this was true.

"Quietly, father took out his jack knife, opened it out and cut the spots away. Mr. Baldwin said, 'Take your horse, Mr. Woolf and go.'

"A few nights before, the boys had gleefully held a pail of wagon grease while Johnny decorated Peter with buttons, gaiter-like, from hock to fetlock.

"But Peter the pony was kept near the wagons at nights from now on, and the wagons night-watched constantly.

"The Indians were very unfriendly and the chief sent word that our stock must be taken off their grazing lands at once. They were told that we intended to move as soon as a suitable crossing to the river could be made, but this did not satisfy them.

"Soon we could see them coming, headed by their chief, all in war paint and feathers.

"It was suggested that now would be a good time for the men to clean their firearms. Father had a pistol, relic of Indian troubles in the early days of Utah. Sterling Williams and Johnny each had a shot gun and there were one or two others in camp.

"The Indians came, but they made no trouble after looking the situation over and seeing that we were able to defend ourselves. However they made frequent visits while the work was in progress of making an approach to the river crossing.

"None seemed friendly or would give information as to the best place for the approach to be made.

"A gravel bar had been located by Johnny under President Card's direction. One of father's wagons was in the lead with two teams of horses attached. Johnny rode one horse of the lead team while father handled the lines.

"There was much debris, and occasionally an uprooted tree came down the muddy stream, but it was not known that the treacherous waters had undermined the river bank at this point causing a jump-off for the horses, and a sudden drop-off for the front wheels.

"The sudden plunge caused an empty two-gallon stone jar in the back of the wagon to fly out at the front, grazing my head and striking one of the horses. There was no time for inquiries or explanations as the hind wheels quickly followed with a jolt.

"Those behind watched with apprehension and all were greatly relieved when the opposite side was reached in safety.

"It was June 1st, at 10 A.M. when Brother Card stopped his team and helped Aunt Zina to alight over the wagon wheel. They stood by a pile of stones. He waved his hat and shouted something which none could hear but all understood.

"Wagons were drawn up while smiling occupants climbed out over the wagon wheels and gave their heartiest salutes: 'Hurrah for Canada!' 'Canada or bust!' 'Three cheers for Canada!'

"Laughter and gladness on every side: Snatches of songs were sung. Each then selected a stone which was added to the fast growing mound which marked the boundary line.

"We had reached the new home land. We were nearing the end of the trail. The new land was indeed an ever-growing source of wonder and delight.

"Sagebrush had been left behind. Instead were wide, rolling prairies covered with tall, waving prairie bunch-grass and wild flowers in profusion — bluebells, yellow sweetpea, Indian paint brush, cranebills and buttercups.

"There was one thing resembling home — the Rocky

Mountains — a wondrous range, with majestic, square-topped Chief Mountain stationed in front as if to give strength and courage to our undertaking.

"There was the morning sun coming up out of the prairie, the lone days, numerous lakes dotting the landscapes, and teeming with a variety of wild fowl.

"We drove north as far as Willow Creek and camped about 2 P.M. at a spot where the Taylorsville school house now stands. Johnny shot two wild ducks. What a welcome change to the bill of fare! It began to rain as soon as camp was made and kept it up all night until about noon on the following day.

"Thursday, June 2nd, was Fast Day; accordingly, fast meeting was held and special prayers offered for our continued safety, especially in crossing the swollen waters of the St. Mary's River. Some Indians had recently drowned in the treacherous and ever-swelling stream.

"Works must ever accompany the faith of these hardy pioneers, so after the prayer meeting they immediately set to work to build a flat-bottomed boat to aid in the crossing. The lumber they had bought was soon converted into a boat.

"On arising at 3 A.M. the following morning, June 3rd, President Card was delighted to find there had been a severe frost during the night. Arousing the camp, an early start was made.

"They were met at St. Mary's River by Sergeant Brimmer of the North-West Mounted Police, who informed them that because of the frost the water had fallen eighteen inches, and that it would not be necessary to use the boat. This word was received with great relief and gratitude, for all felt that an answer to their prayers had been graciously granted by Providence.

"On his excellent mount, Sergeant Brimmer very kindly gave the men all possible assistance.

"The wagon boxes were tied down so they could not float away. Even so, the water ran in, soaking everything. With the sergeant piloting the way, several trips were made with double team each time, crossing and recrossing, until the seven wagons were safely across as well as the stock and drivers. The crossing had been accomplished in four hours at ten A.M., when they were across, it began to rain again.

"They later learned that by sundown of that day the St. Mary's was again at its former high level.

"On they went joyfully, for travelling in the rain was no hardship now as they looked forward to the last lap of the long journey. No more rivers to cross; no more mountains to climb; peace and rest from weary travel was soon to be had for all, after an eight weeks' trip.

"Lee's Creek was just ahead.

"There was now talk of home. 'We'll be home tonight.' 'How good it will seem to be home.' 'Just wait 'til we get home . . .'

"On arriving at the location in the rain, with the long, sodden grass lying flat, the trees drooping and dripping, one wagon box in sight on the ground, on the east side of Lee's Creek, Wilford, aged four, clasped his arms about mother and looking into her face, said woefully, 'Ma, you said we'd be home tonight.'

" 'Yes, dear,' she said. 'This is home from now on.'

"With quivering lips and brimming eyes he asked, 'If this is home, where's all the houses?'

"Mother gazed around too, who can tell with what longing, but bravely and cheerfully she reassured him with promises of a home and happiness until all felt that spirit.

"A new country to subdue, wet weather overhead and

underfoot could not dampen the spirits of that dauntless company . . ."

* * * *

They are gone now, every one.

And on headstone after headstone is carved the one-word epitaph that is the proudest any Albertan can earn: "Pioneer."

LIVING CONDITIONS

"I do not remember living in a tent, as the first year we were here father built a small 2 room log cabin with dirt floors and sod roof with a quilt hung up for a door.

"Conditions were not ideal, but we were very happy."

— Mary Amanda Anderson Layton, pioneer

* * * *

BE IT EVER SO HUMBLE...

Weeks and months of hardships on the trail were bad enough, but they were only beginning for the Alberta pioneer.

Starting with only land and water and sky — and the meagre supplies packed in his wagon — he had to plunge immediately into a struggle for survival.

If he came to ranch, there was a herd to tend day and night; protecting his cattle from wolves and fighting his animals' instinctive tendency to drift back to their old homes again. And he had to persuade the Indians that, despite superficial resemblance, domestic cattle weren't just another breed of buffalo and it wasn't considered good form to hunt them.

If he came to homestead, there was the desperate rush to turn the soil, plant and harvest, so that there would be crops to turn into cash, and food to feed his family.

And, always, the pioneer was goaded by the knowledge of winter's inevitable sweep from the north.

With so much to tend to at first, the pioneer rarely wasted much thought on the issue of a home. A tent or, failing that, the wagon he came in would serve well enough until the pressure was off.

But, sooner or later, the pioneer husband would return to the supper campfire to face a determined wife, pot in hand, wanting to know when she was going to get a house to live in.

Given her determination (and the fact the pot was solid iron) the husband usually found it wise to promise an immediate plunge into the construction industry.

On open prairie, however, it was easier to promise a house than to build one.

For one thing, wood — the key ingredient — was almost always missing. Scrawny willow and aspen were fine for firewood, but they weren't the stuff of the building trade.

To get house-sized logs usually involved a long trek, hard hauling, and time the pioneer didn't have. Lumber was even harder to get — assuming there was a sawmill around at all — and it cost cash he couldn't afford to pay.

So the pioneer wife with visions of a gabled roof and sweeping porch was in for an unpleasant surprise.

If there were a hill somewhere around, she could expect to make her first home in a dug-out: a shallow, man-made cave extended outward with a few poles and a little canvas.

Inside, a low platform raised the bed from the dirt floor. There'd be a crate for a table and an oil lamp for light. An open fire still served as both furnace and cooking range.

Where there wasn't a suitable hill around, the usual alternative was a sod shack.

Foot-thick strips of sod were cut from the prairie, then stacked in a square the way a child makes a tower of blocks. When the shack was high enough, poles were laid across the top and shingled with still more sod. The only openings, usually, were for a door and crude chimney.

Interior furnishings differed little from those of a dugout. The only likely addition was a square metal stove.

The sod shack's efficiency as a house was summed up wryly (by a woman, of course) in 1884:

"On this first visit, Mrs. Shaw laughingly told of waiting in Mr. Barker's cabin with an umbrella held over her to keep dry until the storm subsided.

"The rain inside, under the sod roof, often continued after the storm outside was over . . . ."

There is hardly a pioneer wife in Alberta who doesn't remember at least one winter day in a sod shack, with frozen dirt underfoot and frost seeping in the walls. With smoke swirling from the stove to sting her eyes and a pail of snow waiting to melt.

Wondering, over a coughing child, if freedom doesn't sometimes have too high a price.

* * * *

LACE-TRIMMED CURTAINS COVERED THE WINDOWS . . .

Sooner or later, the pioneer wife got the house she'd asked for in the first place. It often took time — a year or two — and the arrival of enough neighbors for help in its construction. But the day would finally come when she could leave the sod shack behind — maybe stopping long enough to help push down its walls before she did.

One of the best descriptions we have of these first true "houses" comes again from the written history of early Cardston:

"The first homes were alike, built to the square, the gable ends with beams and floor joists. The roofs were covered with rough lumber, tar paper and squares of sod placed closely together.

"The chimneys were five-gallon coal-oil cans fitted in a square hole in the roof through which the stove pipe was thrust.

"The walls were chinked with split timber and plastered inside and out. The floors were made of rough lumber either

sawed with a whipsaw or hauled from Lethbridge with the doors, windows, nails and tar paper.

"The whipsaw was set up on a steep bank on the J.A. Hammer lot. A pit was dug, a log was marked with a string dipped in flour or charcoal and flipped along the length of the log.

"One man operated his end of the saw by standing in the pit, another handled his end from the bank above. Lumber soon began to pile up when it was found that the boards brought from Lethbridge did not suffice.

"All of the men could do carpentering of a sort . . .

"None had reason to be ashamed of his house or furniture, all were so nearly alike and the best to be had at the time — homemade tables, benches, stools, wash benches and corner cupboards nailed to walls.

"For the beds, short lengths of small peeled logs or poles were nailed to walls and floor at the proper height for beds. Poles were fitted and securely nailed to these and bed springs placed on top.

"Where there were not sufficient feather beds or mattresses, bed ticks were filled with straw or hay, placed on the floor at night, or on low trundle beds which were pushed under the stationary bed at night, or on top of another bed.

"For a dressing table three coal-oil cases were used. Two, upended with shelves and with a third laid on its side across the top, left a space between where another small box could be placed.

"Half of the top box had a hinged lid. Covered with curtains and a lace-trimmed scarf, these could be made to look very dainty and were exceedingly useful. Candles, coal oil lamps, and various toilet articles were put on top and a mirror hung on the wall above.

"Nearly every family had brought with them engraved

or enlarged family portraits, daguerrotypes and tin-types of family and relatives left behind. These were hung on the walls or placed on the improvised dresser tops. Some brought their choice hair flowers in shadow-box frames to decorate the walls.

"The floors were covered with home-woven rag carpets over layers of clean wheat straw, and those lucky enough to obtain buffalo robes from the Indians spread these on the floor on which children could tumble about. These were also used as laprobes in the winter.

"Homespun, lace-trimmed curtains covered the windows. All the lace was hand-made.

"Wood-burning stoves had four holes, a wide removable hearth in front which hid the ashes from view. The oven doors swung outward and were fastened with a latch. There were no reservoirs or warming ovens.

"These were soon replaced with coal ranges and new utensils replaced the heavy iron pots, bake ovens and skillets, the brass buckets, and wooden tubs."

* * * *

BEHIND EVERY WELL-FED MAN ...

"The women were all experts at making a variety of breads such as salt-rising, graham gems, cornmeal Johnny cake, pancakes and biscuits made with buttermilk and soda, and now that the potatoes were dug and stored they once again had their delicious potato-yeast bread." (Recollections of a pioneer — female)

"The bread was fried and, of course, it was as hard as wood. After setting until the next meal, it was so hard you

could knock a cow down with it." (Recollections of anoth-er pioneer — male)

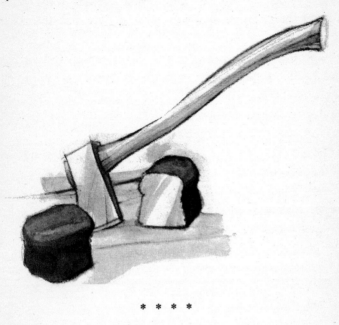

* * * *

A WORD FROM THE KITCHEN . . .

Pioneer women sometimes complain that historians (male historians, that is) give the impression that the west was won by man alone.

Not so, argue those like Dora Trew of Lethbridge. If the man was in front, she claims, the woman was never more than a step or two behind — and usually dragging a stone-boat to boot.

Discussing the life of the pioneer woman, she paints a fascinating picture of domesticity in a growing Alberta:

"A typical kitchen in those days centred, of course, around the cooking range with its warm-air oven above, its tank of hot water attached to one side, its coal-bucket close by. Coal was not too hard to find in the south; it sometimes could be dug out of the side of a coulee, or obtained around the vicinity of Lethbridge. If the bucket was empty, one could go out onto flat prairie and gather 'buffalo chips'.

"Nearby was the big table with its chairs or benches and beside the door, because it was handiest for filling, stood the barrel of water with its long-handled dipper. There was the broom, the big tin tub, the laundry wash-boiler hanging on the wall, and the modest coal oil can, its long spout stopped with a small potato.

"There was usually a cot or bed squeezed in somewhere. In one corner stood the triangular shelf with its wash basin, beside it the roller towel, that handy, rolling symbol of a heroic age, that played such an important part along with the canned tomato and dried apple.

"If the women lived on the prairie as most of them did in the beginning, the water usually had to be hauled from a river or well on a stone-boat.

"This was a contraption with a flat platform on heavy runners, that did double duty by hauling away stones when clearing the land. It was dragged easily enough over the prairie grass, but where would you find a place for it today?

"Water was so valuable that it was mostly used for cooking and drinking, though of course one had to wash occasionally.

"For the family laundry the housewife had the pleasure in winter of hauling in snow and melting it in the big copper boiler where the clothes were boiled, and afterwards scrubbed on a washboard. However, these clothes flapping on the line (or on the fence) were something to be admired.

"In the small towns that grew up there developed the 'water-man' who hauled water from the river in tanks. In Lethbridge, for instance, it was delivered three times a week at a cost of $2 per month.

"In winter he seemed a replica of the modern Wizard of Oz as he staggered up the yard, a pail of water in each hand, making a silken rustling sound as he walked. From his coat and elbows hung snapping icicles and the drips from his pails froze instantly into little round balls.

"Finally he would reach the back door, sloshing into the kitchen with a big blast of cold air, spilling as he went, and always with a cheery word for everyone as he turned away.

"But of course all this improved as time went on. Finally came the waterworks in small towns. In Lethbridge it appeared from the taps in the spring break-up as a sort of thin mud. It was cleared for drinking by settling with alum, then boiled to settle the germs, and by this time was nasty enough to settle anyone but an old-timer.

"I can recall the horrified expression on the face of an aunt from England when mother nonchalantly turned a thick, steaming mass of this gruel into the bathtub.

"At about this period our waterworks became out of order until an enterprising plumber found, and removed, from the tank, the remains of a fish.

"Pioneer white women did not have too much to do with that horror, pemmican, but some of them had their experiences with the unpalatable stone-like bun called 'hardtack'. It was made of flour, water, and salt, fried or baked, and, like pemmican, was sometimes served with an axe. There were such luxuries as beans and 'larup', a sort of light molasses which provided sweetness, and occasionally there were dried fruits.

"However, after the early days of buffalo meat, there were many splendid dishes made savory by being cooked in iron utensils.

"The cellar was usually well-stocked with foods by autumn. In our home, we managed to get rid of a whole ton of potatoes, not to mention two barrels of apples, which around 1900 were sent out yearly from 'down east'. Eggs were preserved in big crocks of lime or dipped in boiling water, wrapped and stored . . ."

* * * *

MEANWHILE AT THE COSMOPOLITAN . . .

If the Alberta pioneer ever found home fare dull, well, he could always take a run into a town like Medicine Hat, tie up at the Cosmopolitan Hotel, and have a meal that would — judging from the Christmas menu that follows — more than satisfy any appetite.

Russian Caviar on Toast

Chiffonade Celery	White Onions
Green House Lettuce	Queen Olive
Sliced Tomatoes	Sliced Cucumbers

SOUPS
Potage Alexandrine   Consomme Renaissance

FISH
Boiled B.C. Halibut and White Sauce
Boiled Columbia Sole and Genoise Sauce
(Wafer Potatoes)

SWEET ENTREES
King Apple in Sponge Ring
New York Chocolate Eclair & Rignet Sauce

Rabbit Cutlets Breaded and Calf's Head Sauce
Young Pigeon, aux Gelee
Broiled Oysters, Maitre de Hotel

BOILED
Sugar Cured Ham and Champagne Sauce
Sheep's Tongue au Gelee
Boiled Chicken and Almond Sauce

ROASTS
Young Alberta Turkey, Marjral Dressing
and Cranberry Sauce (Weaners)
Tenderloin of Beef and Yorkshire Pudding
Suckling Pig and Sauce Pomme
Spring Chicken and Bourginotte Sauce
Mallard Duck and Crab Apple Jelly
Roast Goose and Walnut Dressing

COLD MEATS
Turkey   Chicken   Goose   Duck   Ham
Ox Tongue

VEGETABLES
Steamed Potatoes   Lyonnaise Potatoes
Mashed Potatoes
French Green Peas   Wax Beans

SALADS
Russian Salad   Shrimp Salad   Hamard Salad
Fruit Salad

RELISHES

Lee and Perrin's Sauce   Mixed Pickles

Sweet Pickles   Chow Chow

Tomato Catsup   Pickled Beets

Pickled Walnuts

PUDDING

English Plum Pudding with Cognac or Hard Sauce

COLD SWEETS

Fruit Trifle   Fruit Pudding

PASTRY

Deep Apple Pie with Whipped Cream

Boston Cream Pie   Hot Mince Pie

Citron Tart

For those hardy enough to continue, the menu goes on to list 11 varieties of cakes, six varieties of jellies and a whole host of "desserts."

The wine list includes Champagne (Mumm's Extra Dry), Claret (Julien), Port Wine, Dry Catawba and St. Augustine.

The Cosmopolitan's price for permission to tackle the feast was one slim dollar. Wine (and bicarbonate of soda) extra, of course.

* * * *

For most of the earlier settlers, of course, a feast at the Cosmo — even at $1 — was a luxury hopelessly out of reach. Many didn't have a dollar, and even those who did couldn't leave ranch or homestead untended that long.

So it was left to the ingenuity of the prairie wife to make a feast of what could be grown or hunted. Sometimes, as the following ditty of the period illustrates, she didn't succeed:

> "Rabbits young, rabbits old
> Rabbits hot, rabbits cold
> Rabbits tender, rabbits tough
> Thank you Sir, I've had enough"

* * * *

LONELY TIME, PARTY TIME . . .

Sen. F.W. Gershaw, recalling the lives of the pioneers, paints a bleak picture of conditions in early Alberta:

"Married men usually went alone, and got their families out when they had some accommodation. There were many difficulties. Water was scarce, the flies were bad, stores were far away and money was scarce. The roof often leaked and wood or coal was very hard to obtain.

"The settlers were lonesome and often discouraged. The women in particular deserve great credit for the heroic way they lived. They kept the homes, managed to prepare food and taught the children. They read the Bible and tried to maintain their religious beliefs. They would walk miles to help a neighbor in trouble.

"Some of the bachelor homesteaders developed mental trouble. Loneliness, poor food, worry and lack of cleanliness on account of water being so hard to get, in some cases, caused a departure from the normal way of acting.

"It was a hard life . . ."

Oh, it was a hard life all right. But not so hard, as Sen. Gershaw acknowledges, that a man forgot how to laugh.

And there wasn't a man or woman in pioneer Alberta

whose toe didn't start tapping to the sound of a fiddle, or who wouldn't struggle into a boiled shirt or a thick layer of petticoats at the prospect of a party.

And early Albertans could turn anything from the opening of a church hall to the raising of a barn into a party.

"They'd come from as far as 50 miles away," muses one pioneer, "with bull teams, buckboards, prairie schooners, buggies, or on horseback.

"Max Broulette fiddling away; John Smith, master of ceremonies calling out his hoarse commands from a point of vantage on a packing box.

"Many of the men were married to Indian women; the women arriving in their best print dresses, on their backs the babies which were blanketed and stowed away under seats or benches.

"It was not an uncommon joke for some of the young cowboys to change the wrappings on these bundles of young natives and when the mothers returned home they would discover they had the wrong offspring!

"The big social event of the year was the military ball given by the NWMP, attended by people from all over Alberta.

"The ladies, fashionably dressed in their silk gowns, and the red-coated Mounties in full dress, made a gay sight as they danced the lancers, the military schottische, the ripple waltz, mazurka or three-step . . ."

* * * *

SO I SAYS TO THE QUEEN . . .

Pioneer Albertans had dozens of ways to entertain themselves in the inevitable intervals between dances, but no way was more popular than story-telling.

Probably the undisputed champion in this department was Fred Stimson, owner of the famous Bar-U Ranch in High River.

In 1887, it seems, he went to London to attend the celebrations connected with Queen Victoria's Jubilee:

"Well, boys," Fred said, propping his feet up on the bunkhouse stove, "on my arrival in London I went straight to the Hotel Cecil and had scarcely got nicely settled in my quarters when a bellhop came and said I was wanted on the telephone.

"I went at once to the booth and took up the receiver. A sweet-voiced woman said, 'Is that Mr. Fred Stimson, of High River, Alberta, Canada?' to which I replied that my name and address were quite correct.

"I nearly dropped dead with surprise when I was next informed that it was Queen Victoria speaking. I was so flabbergasted that I could only say: 'Oh, your Majesty! I have often heard of you.'

"But she put me quite at ease by saying, 'And I have very often been informed of you and your doings in the far West, Mr. Stimson. I hear that you are stopping at the Cecil?'

" 'Yes, your Majesty,' I replied, 'and I am very comfortable.'

" 'No doubt you are, Mr. Stimson, but I should like you to visit us at Buckingham Palace, and as we have rooms to burn here, I shall send the carriage for you.'

"With this she rang off. I knew of course, that a royal invitation was a command and I had scarcely got my traps together when I chanced to look out of the window. My heart nearly stopped beating when I saw the royal coach drawn by four white horses with outriders and postilions standing in front of the hotel.

"You should have seen the flunkies of the Cecil dance

attendance on me — they took me for some pumpkins, I can tell you.

"We drove at once to Buckingham Palace, and who should meet me at the door but Queen Victoria herself. She told off a couple of servants in livery to convey my luggage to a suite of rooms reserved for me.

"You ought to have seen the wonderful paintings and Oriental rugs that you sank into when you walked on them, and a bed with a canopy over it and all of the other gorgeous things that you see in a palace.

"Well, boys, it was all very fine for a time, but after a while it began to pall on me so I went down town to see the sights and falling in with some Canadian visitors in London, I stayed out pretty late.

"Next morning at breakfast the Queen, who had come to know me pretty well by this time, said, 'Fred, you were a little late in getting home last night.'

" 'Yes, your Majesty,' I said, 'I met in with some western friends and — ' but she cut me short with 'Oh yes, I understand, boys will be boys, but for your convenience I shall see that you are supplied with a latch-key.'

"Well, I received the key and carried it about with me, but a few evenings later, when strolling down Picadilly, I ran into a bunch of Alberta boys and we made a night of it. I got back to Buckingham at about three a.m. and fiddled around with the latch key for a time.

"Presently I heard a window overhead go up and a soft voice called out, 'Is that you, Fred?'

"Recognizing it at once as that of the Queen, I replied, 'It is, your Majesty, I have the latch-key all right, but I can't find the keyhole.'

" 'Never mind,' said she, 'just wait until I put on my crown and I'll come down and let you in.'

"And sure enough," Fred concluded with appropriate solemnity, "she did."

* * * *

THE DECEASED CAME TO HER DEATH . . .

If some men were good at telling a story, there were others who were just as good at providing the real-life material for one. Such a man was Jack Symonds, one of the early members of the North-West Mounted Police.

John D. Higinbotham of Lethbridge writes of running into the good Mr. Symonds at Wood Mountain detachment in the early 1880's.

"Jack," explains Mr. Higinbotham, "acted as cook and batman for 'Paper Collar Johnnie,' as Inspector A.R. Macdonnell was irreverently nick-named, and took fearsome liberties with his master's food.

"Whenever beefsteak was to be cooked for breakfast Jack usually prepared (?) it by tossing it upon the kitchen floor and jumping on it with his long boots, and then throwing it against the walls or ceiling before putting it in the frying-pan.

"These culinary liberties, or eccentricities, were, fortunately for Jack, not reported to the Inspector or solitary confinement on bread and water might have been his portion."

Jack Symonds brought his cooking career to its climax in an incident that made him story-material all over Alberta — and came close to costing him his neck.

It was touched off by the sudden death of an Indian woman on the Blood Reserve, and the verdict handed down by the coroner's jury. The written decision tells the whole story:

"That the deceased came to her death . . . by poison administered by John Symonds, of the North-West Mounted Police, OR ELSE by eating too large a quantity of sour beans."

Although there were some who grumbled that Jack's cooking made the first alternative more than likely, the verdict's "or else" saved his skin.

* * * *

And, of course, there was many a green-horn or remittance man who went away convinced by the solemn assurance of an Alberta pioneer that the rags hung on fences by survey teams were really large handkerchiefs for the cattle to blow their noses.

Oh yes, this new land of Alberta was tough country all right. And the people who tamed it had to put up with leaky cabins and poor food and every other variety of hardship.

But they never forgot how to laugh.

RANGE RIDERS

PISTOL PERSUASION . . .

John Ware, the famous Negro cowboy and foreman of the Bar-U Cattle Company, was away when the two strangers rode onto the spread.

The pair found owner Fred Stimson and demanded the return of a horse they claimed they had raised, but which now bore the brand of the Bar-U.

Stimson, a deceptively mild-mannered man, was enraged at the suggestion he was a horse thief, but he chose not to show it. Instead he decided to try the course of sweet reason, and listened politely as the two armed and angry men described the animal they had come to get.

Finally, Stimson saddled up and led the two out to where the ranch horses were grazing. He sat quietly as his visitors again laid adamant claim to a white gelding, then just as quietly pointed out the animal's mother which, like the gelding in question, had been raised from birth on the Bar-U.

The strangers, growing uglier by the minute, insisted they were going to take the horse anyway.

At that moment, John Ware came riding up. Stimson turned to him:

"John, you know this gelding we call Billy?"

Ware nodded. "Yes sir, I sure do. We brought him up from a colt. What of it?"

"Well, John, these two gentleman claim that he belongs to them. What are we going to do about it?"

Ware's hand blurred across his holster and before the two startled strangers knew what had happened they were taking turns looking down the barrel of the foreman's .45 Colt. There was an ominous click as Ware cocked back the hammer.

"Shall I kill 'em now, boss," Ware asked softly, "or will I wait until they take the horse?"

Not anxious to hear Stimson's answer, the strangers abruptly wheeled their horses and fled in a cloud of dust.

* * * *

WITH HOPE AND A REPEATING RIFLE . . .

The age of the open range in Alberta didn't last that long — only the 32 years from 1880 to 1912 — but it lasted long enough to create the particular stamp of outlook and temperament that marks an Albertan today.

Determination and self-reliance are still important qualities, and big factors in a province that hasn't stopped changing and growing.

But in 1880, determination and self-reliance weren't just important. They were vitally necessary if a man was going to survive in Alberta.

In Montana and Texas, by 1880, civilization in its least desirable forms was beginning to catch up with the cattleman. Precious range land was being cropped bare by flocks of sheep, and it was being cut away by the fences of newly-arrived farmers.

It seemed there just wasn't room for a rancher in the U.S.A. anymore.

More and more, cowmen found themselves staring north-ward to the rolling grasslands of southern Alberta. And, more and more, they were deciding to "try their luck" in an unsettled land.

It was a tempting gamble. And, thanks to Chinooks and good grass — and a healthy injection of British capital — it was going to pay off.

In 1880, of course, no one knew anything certain about any pay-off. All they knew about was the gamble itself.

Sure there were Chinooks. But Chinooks — in those areas where they came at all — were still only intervals in cold and stormy winters. And even good grass dries out in summers when there is no rain.

Nor was nature all that the pioneer rancher had to worry about. Open range land was an invitation to rustlers and horse-thieves, Indians had been made hostile by whiskey traders and wolfers, and police were few and far between.

It was the era of Mutiny Fleming; of young Jack De-Haven, rifle in one hand and pistol in the other, fleeing the law on both sides of the U.S.–Canadian border; and of Kid Currie on his blueberry roan — wanted for shooting the sheriff of a Montana town.

And, in 1891 at High River, Harry Longbaugh — the Sundance Kid — was breaking horses for a railroad con-tractor, and getting occasional visits from a friend by the name of Robert Le Roy Parker, alias Butch Cassidy.

The "law" of the range was a set of quick wits, a re-peating rifle, and a fast hand with a Colt pistol.

* * * *

RANCHING THE BORDER COUNTRY . . .

Unlike most of the other pioneer ranchers in the border country of southeast Alberta, Bill Mitchell didn't speak with the twang of Montana or Texas. Rather, he spoke with the soft burr of his Kippen, Scotland birthplace.

Bill was a boy of 10 when he and his family had their first taste of Alberta ranching at Elkwater Lake in 1888. There the youngster quickly learned how dearly pioneer ranchmen paid for their gambles in the unknown of the border country.

Years later, he could still recall the prairie fires that threatened to destroy the ranch time and time again. He remembered the timber wolves that prowled the calf sheds, and he remembered the bear-mauled carcass of a doe whose fawn he carried home and fed from a baby bottle.

Most vividly of all, he remembered the winter, one of his first in Canada, when hundreds of cattle perished in the deep snow. In the spring he watched the cattle that survived buckle under their own weight and lie helpless until ranch hands could come and put them out of their misery with rifle bullets.

Bill Mitchell watched carefully and learned, better than most, the lessons nature was teaching.

He was also quick to learn anything the shrewd cowboys on the ranch had to teach him.

"When I was 14," he recalled in an interview a couple of years before his death in 1946, "I'd ridden with Michel Quesnel (a former NWMP scout working as a horse-breaker at Elkwater) after Indians who'd run off with a bunch of the horses.

"Michel lost no time, and he knew his business. When we were leaving father told him to notify the Willow Creek detachment.

"Michel grunted a reply and we started up the old mill road behind the house, although the tracks showed they'd gone west toward the Medicine Lodge.

"He never intended going near the detachment, but rode straight south. We picked up their trail in Willow Creek and started crowding them hard.

" 'Indian cayuses have bad time driving that bunch,' he chuckled. 'We catch up leetle while now. They see us, then vamoose.'

"He was right. They only got away with two gentle saddle ponies they were able to catch. We rounded up the others under a cutbank and Michel roped two with a new rawhide lariat I'd helped him plait, and we started for home on fresh horses.

" 'Never waste time notifying police — git goin' yourself,' was his advice then, and I decided to follow it . . ."

Bill Mitchell was a good student. At 17, he staked squatter's rights on Willow Creek and was in business as owner of the LA Ranch — right in the middle of the best winter-grazing land in Alberta.

Three years later, Bill's father died, and left him heir to the Elkwater ranch, and heir to the responsibilities of caring for a large family of younger brothers and sisters.

Remembering the fate of the cattle at Elkwater, Bill moved all the stock to Willow Creek and turned the old ranch into a feed operation.

The Willow Creek ranch quickly became the rendezvous of cowpunchers for hundreds of miles around.

He remembered thousands of cattle grazing the hills and coulees. They came in from as far north as the Bow River. Many were "drifted" in by Montana ranchers who had been "sheeped out" and were poaching on the rich Canadian grass and winter range.

Everywhere, Mitchell recalled, you could see long-legged Texas steers with the horn-spread of a moose. Wild and wily with age, they were almost impossible to catch as they raced off at the first sight of a man on horseback.

Roundups were massive affairs, and cowboys criss-crossed the territory with pack-horse, branding iron and lariat — branding the calf crop where they found it.

Maverick cattle were considered the property of the first man to run a brand on them. Usually they were slaughtered for the chuck-wagon or sold to help defray operating expenses.

Cattle rustling, brand-working and butchering were all considered a form of free enterprise as long as they were confined to American stock. "After all," Bill Mitchell said explaining the rationale behind the practice, "ain't we feedin' the critters — thousands of 'em — free?"

The NWMP took a different view, but in so large a territory enforcement was all but impossible.

American beef finished on Canadian grass, grinned Bill Mitchell, "was shore toothsome."

And, as he pointed out, it wasn't all one way. Montana outfits were just as handy at drifting Canadian beef across the line during their fall round-ups.

The rugged border country between southeastern Alberta and Montana was ready-made for cattle rustlers and horse thieves.

Very often, Bill Mitchell explained, the Montana rustlers had confederates on the Canadian side of the border — "Sometimes they turned out to be fellows who had their feet under your table most of the time."

What made the situation intolerable for Alberta ranchers was the attitude across the border. In Montana there was a vigilante committee that "strung up" anyone preying on

Montana ranchers. But as far as the U.S.A. was concerned, rustlers had a free hand on the Canadian side of the line and once cattle had crossed the border there was little chance of recovery.

The NWMP, on the other hand, was diligent about returning any stock rustled from the U.S. side.

The policy of the Alberta rancher faced with a case of Montana rustlers, explained Mitchell, was "git after them yourself."

Not long after he started the LA Ranch, Mitchell was raided by horse thieves and, remembering the advice of old Michel Quesnel, he put the "git after them yourself" philosophy into practice.

He had a hunch the thieves were a Montana bunch known as the Bear Paws' Gang, and he rode hard to a cabin he knew they used. It was dark when he arrived.

"The lamp was lit when I rode up to the door. I recognized one of the men and walked in.

" 'I've come for my horses,' I told him. His eyes fairly popped. Then he shrugged, 'All right, kid, you win. They're in the corral and damn tired — the wild buggers.' "

It wasn't to be the last time Bill Mitchell would have to step boldly into possible trouble with outlaws. But, as he recalled years later, it wasn't outlaws who were responsible for the only two times in his life he was in serious danger; it was the weather.

The first time had come when he was only a boy and he and his brother had nearly perished in a blizzard. They survived only by the accident of running into a haystack in the storm.

The second time came years after his run-in with the Bear Paws' Gang.

Mitchell was riding along the Milk River alone when he

went snow blind. With all sense of direction lost, he had to trust his life to the instincts of his horse. On open range, a horse given his head would head home or to a place where he'd been frequently stabled.

Mitchell hoped fervently it would be the latter. The LA Ranch was 40 miles away.

"I tied a knot in the lines, and hung them over the pommel, giving my horse his head.

"For a long time he didn't go off a walk, but I could tell by the way he was feeling his way we were in rough country. Probably in the badlands and headed for the detachment at Pen d'Oreille — or maybe Spencer Bros.

"Then he started hazing along at a steady walking trot. He was evidently on a bare ridge, and from his blowing snorts I knew he was contented, and was on his way to stable and oats.

"After a while he slowed to a walk, stopped, snorted and turned back. When it happened a third time I figured he was looking for a way down a cutbank. I was right, and it was surely steep.

"Next there was a yelping of many dogs. Indians, b'gad! I picked up the lines and turned him toward the barking. A strong Indian lifted me off and helped me into a teepee. It was warm and smelled of kin-a-kin-ic and wood fire.

"I knew a little Cree and was able to make him understand to bring in my saddle. He spread my saddle blanket over me. It was still warm.

"The woman gave me a can of what tasted like sage tea, and put a warm pad on my eyes. It smelled like soaked buffalo grass and sure felt good.

"I drank a lot of the tea but I couldn't bring myself to the dog mulligan. Not for a long time. But finally I grew such an appetite I'd have eaten the old buck himself if he'd been in the pot.

"The morning I left I gave him what money I had — $7 or $8 maybe. Not much for all their care and kindness, but it bought a lot of flour in those days.

"Oh, yes, I was covered with fleas all right, but rearin' and prancin' like a grain-fed bronc.

It was no wonder that Bill Mitchell always fought the theory that wandering bands of Indians were to blame for killing beef. He always maintained that the real culprits were white men hiding behind the plight of hungry natives.

And to the end of his days, Bill Mitchell was always arguing — with a grin — that dog mulligan was "dashed good eating at that!"

* * * *

STILL MORE FROM MR. STIMSON . . .

Not even so serious a business as rustling can keep the western sense of humor hidden for long.

Again it is Fred Stimson of the Bar-U who proves that even a court of law isn't immune from frontier wit.

Stimson's Bar-U was prosecuting a man for misbranding one of their cattle, and the defendant had hired walrus-shaped Paddy Nolan (the Alberta lawyer who was one of the best criminal lawyers in Canadian history) to act for him.

Stimson, as chief witness for the Crown, was in the witness box:

Mr. Nolan: "Your name is Frederick Stimson, I believe?"
Mr. Stimson: "It is, sir."
Mr. Nolan: "You spend most of your time riding the range, do you not?"
Mr. Stimson: "No, sir, I spend most of my time in bed."

Mr. Nolan: "You are very short-sighted, I believe, Mr. Stimson?"

Mr. Stimson: "No, sir, I am not."

Mr. Nolan: "Then why do you wear glasses?"

Mr. Stimson: "Oh, just for effect."

Mr. Nolan: "Now, Mr. Stimson, you claim that my client misbranded one of your cattle?"

Mr. Stimson: "I do, sir."

Mr. Nolan: "Please describe the animal to the Court?"

Mr. Stimson: "Well, it was an ordinary, everyday steer with a leg on each corner."

Mr. Nolan: (disgusted at not making any headway with the witness) "I believe, Mr. Stimson, that you regard yourself as something of a smart aleck?"

Mr. Stimson: "I am also informed that you do a little smart alecking yourself."

Mr. Nolan: (thoroughly exasperated) "That will do, Mr. Stimson. Your Lordship, I am through with the witness."

* * * *

NOW, ABOUT THAT DRINK . . .

Cowboy humor was honed in that toughest of arenas, the bunkhouse. And unfortunate indeed was the greenhorn who set himself up for a sample of it — particularly if the greenhorn was one of those frontier rarities, a travelling salesman.

The travelling salesman, stiff-collared and perspiring, was hanging over the bar and holding forth with excitement at seeing his first herd of buffalo.

Trying to stir some enthusiasm in his straight-faced cowboy audience, he offered to set up the drinks if anyone present had seen more than 100,000 buffalo at one time.

One of the audience, a famous joker, promptly volunteered the information that he had seen "a hundred million billion blessed buffalo at one time."

The salesman demanded details, not noticing the other cowboys were red-faced with the strain of not laughing, and the joker was delighted to comply.

He spun a tale of horror in which he and a troop of 50 men had been caught for five days in a bufflalo stampede and each man fired his rifle steadily during that time to keep the troop from being run over.

"And finally," he told the pop-eyed drummer, "there was a break and we got across a river and up on a hill.

"It was a good job we did, because from there we could see the main body of buffalo coming."

* * * *

GOT EWE! . . .

Occasionally, if we can believe yet another cowboy tale, the greenhorn didn't always come out second-best in ex-exchanges of humor with ranch hands.

Even though one can't help but be a little suspicious when the victim is a sheep rancher, the following story at least suggests the westerner was prepared to laugh at himself now and then:

The sheep rancher, despite grave misgivings, had broken down and hired a young British remittance man to work as a hand on the ranch.

Determined to test the foppish young gentleman early, the rancher assigned him the chore of rounding up a flock of sheep about a mile from the ranch house.

The young man seemed hesitant, and when pressed, admitted he didn't know what a sheep looked like. The rancher, rolling his eyes, pointed out that sheep are white and fuzzy and "Maybe I'd better send another man and a dog out with you to make sure you get them in."

The remittance man drew himself up to full height and thanked the rancher coldly, but added: "Won't really be necessary, sir. Quite capable of handling the little blighters myself. At Eton I attained some fame for my fleetness of foot, etc. and I'm sure I am quite capable."

The rancher pointed his new hand in the right direction and sat back to wait for results.

Hour followed hour and still the young man did not return Finally, with the sun about to set, the rancher grew alarmed and prepared to set out in search of the greenhorn.

Just then, the remittance man, bedraggled and panting, stumbled in the door.

"I did my best, sir," he told the astonished rancher with visible anguish, "but try as I might I could only run down half a dozen of the little devils."

And, with that, he handed the rancher six struggling jack rabbits.

* * * *

HERE, PRINCE . . .

Western hospitality is legendary — almost as legendary as western informality.

It is doubtful that in any part of the world but Alberta would one illustrious newcomer have been given quite as casual an introduction:

"Prince, meet Billy-the-Buster. Billy, meet Prince."

"Howdy, Prince."

"Good afternoon, Mr. Billy-the-Buster," responded His Royal Highness, Edward, The Prince of Wales, with a barely-suppressed grin.

* * * *

ROUND-UP DAYS . . .

Most of the old cowboys are gone now. Only a few remain who can feel the warm tug of recollection when someone like the late Bill Mitchell writes of the bunkhouse where Michel Quesnel would wring lively French-Canadian tunes from a battered accordion while his saddle-mates plaited lariats, filled cartridges and moulded bullets in preparation for another day on the range.

One of the last survivors of that era is Bud Cotton, who now lives in Calgary. A talented wood-carver and a literate writer, Mr. Cotton is filled with chuckling memories of the years when he rode "night hawk", herding the saddle horses through the hours from dusk to dawn, on the Pat Burns spread.

"During the fall roundups," he explains, "on a real frosty morning, those cow ponies always had a hump in their backs, and no matter how hard you hauled up on the old latigo strap (the strap for tightening the saddle girth), the saddle seemed never to lie down.

"The cowpoke, with the chill of dawn in his bones and kinks in his frame from bedding down on the hard prairie, didn't feel at all anxious to fork old Dobbin, who was watching his every move with a malevolent eye.

"Sometimes, talking sweet nothings in the bronc's ear and easing gently into the saddle, you could coax him out of camp without getting the coffee and bacon riled up too bad. Camp scenes at dawn were always interesting at any time of the year.

"The summer of 1912 found us camping at the Indian Head spring on the Blackfoot reservation. It was one of the P. Burns outfits, with Jack Monahan as wagon boss.

"There were 75-odd head of saddle broncs in our string and about 25 head of a rep string which brought the cavvies (saddle horses) up to a hundred, including the old bell mare.

"The chuckwagon was manned by our prize cook, Lee Quong. Don't know where Jack Monahan picked him up, but Lee sure was a good cook. He had been with the outfit for years. Many a hunk of pie and swig of java he has left out for me, the night hawk, in case it should be possible for me to slip in during the long night of riding herd on the wandering cavvie.

"Ask any of the old cowmen and they'll tell you, 'Sure we knew Jack Monahan.' He had been with the Burns outfit for over 30 years and to me, then a young punk, he was one of the best.

"Dawn would just be creeping over the ridges with wisps of fog still hanging around camp as I ran the cavvie into the rope corral strung up from the camp wagon. Jack would be waiting there with his rawhide coiled, and despite the fact that he had lost one hand in an accident, he would rope out the saddle string for the day's ride with never a miss.

"Sometimes I'd get in late with the bunch — and when I say late I mean about 6 a.m. — noticing I'd lost four or five head during the dark hours. On dark wet nights especially, it was hard to keep track of the cavvie. They roamed all night, and that meant sitting in the saddle and drifting with the bunch until daylight. By then you might be miles from camp. It was a case of rounding up what horses you had and hitting it for camp pronto, as the boys would be waiting.

"Jack would just seem to glance over the cavvie. 'Now where in hell is that J Flag bay? You been sleeping again, boy? Well, you brought in that old bell mare anyhow. You get some grub from Lee and hit out and hunt those lost horses.'

"The cow waddies (cow-punchers) that were on Jack's crew that summer, Sam Brown and Phil Bozart — Missouri — were top hands. Also included were Scotty Ross, Clem Hanson, Powder River and Jim Finch. Art, a Yank from Fort Worth, wrangled the horses during the day and an Indian by the name of Red Blanket also rode with the outfit — that is, when he and Jim Finch were not too busy trading horses and camp bacon.

"I remember it was that summer we had to ford a bunch of cows and calves across the Bow, the ferry having gone out during the high water a few days before, and we were having one hell of a time trying to get them started, for the calves would balk at the water's edge and mother cow would run back.

"Missouri, on a bet, chucked his clothes and swam across the cold, swift-running Bow, which was nearly half a mile wide at this point and tough swimming too. He was carried downstream quite a way but made it and brought back an old rowboat.

"This we loaded with some of the bawling calves. Their frantic mammies edged into the river trying to reach their infants and were soon swimming out and acting as leaders. We had the whole outfit swimming across the Bow.

"I can still remember how cold the water was, and how scared I was as some of the cattle, turning in the swift current, had riders and doggies all mixed up in the churning mess as we landed on the south bank.

"Another good cowpoke was Powder River — I never knew his real name — a local cowpoke, happy-go-lucky as they make them and always in trouble.

"I remember the morning I had brought in the saddle bunch and corraled them. Jack Monahan, roping out the mounts, snaked out a big wild-eyed black and turned it over to Powder River, then went into his pup tent.

"Mornings were chilly and the saddle just stuck cantle-up on that black's kinked back no matter how hard Powder pulled on the latigoes. You could tell by the look in the black's eye that he did not feel like working for any ornery cowhand that day.

"Powder's horse had loped into the camp just before dawn so I knew he had been in town pretty well all night and was feeling none too gentle about life in general.

"So here was a real set-up for action. Two ornery critters, cowboy and bronc, open range; no stampede rules; no holds barred.

"The bronc bucked through his repertoire. There were times that too much daylight was showing under Powder's pants, but he stuck, and the Black seemed to be determined not to leave camp, so he bucked through the bunch in the corrals, round the wagons and over tent ropes, and finally into and Over Jack Monahan's sacred tent.

"From Jack's remarks it looked as if Powder's days on the NL wagon were done. Jack figured Powder had done it on purpose and steered that bucking black into his tent just to be ornery. But by the next day it was all forgotten.

"Jim Finch was another of the boys — an old cow waddie from Amarillo, Texas way; old but awfully tough, with tales of long trails and gunsmoke in the southwest.

"Jack Monahan once sent Jim into Gleichen for a side of bacon when Lee, the cook, was short, figuring that Jim was a staid old puncher that could be trusted, and not like us unstable punks.

"Jim came back into camp that night wearing a grin, but no bacon tied to his saddle. It would be in the next day he said, but this happened three days running.

"Jack got suspicious and decided to take a trip into

town himself to investigate. He learned that Jim, the trust-worthy, had left town each day with a side of bacon but en-route had traded off the bacon for jugs of Red Eye.

"Red Blanket, the Indian who was a day wrangler, found one of Jim's cached jugs, sampled it, and that afternoon tore through camp like a howling dervish, horse cavvie and all, uttering wild war whoops until he fell off and went to sleep.

"Jim stayed with us, but he hated anyone who mentioned bacon. Red Blanket was sent home to his hogan in disgrace."

Bud Cotton sighs and shakes his head. "Gone are those old cow wagon days," he muses. "Gone, too, the old open range where we used to roam the tough, rough old cow trails of yesterday . . ."

* * * *

THE BIG GAMBLE OF 1903 . . .

It was the winter of 1902-1903 and, even though the era of the open range had only nine years left to run, Alberta ranchers were convinced it would last forever.

As winter broke into an early spring, ranchers — with unconscious unanimity — decided to stake everything they had on the biggest gamble of their lives.

Had the gamble paid off, who knows what Alberta's ranching industry would be like today.

But it didn't pay off. In a tragic seven days in May, Alberta cattlemen lost virtually everything they had, and ranching here changed forever.

Never before had the range been as green in the short grass country of southern Alberta as it was that early spring. The grass rolled on endlessly, as far as the eye could see — hundreds of thousands of acres of it still unscarred by barbwire fences and untouched by plough.

Everywhere, springs bubbled full, sloughs and water-holes were filled to overflowing.

Grass and water, slough hay, an early spring and expanding markets. It was a rancher's paradise — and it was all free.

It was the ranchman's chance to make a killing. The country was opening up. Division of the North West Territories into provinces was a foregone conclusion now, and a great development period loomed ahead for the west.

There would be legislative buildings going up, railways and roads to be built, settlements and schools. Beef and more beef would be in demand for construction crews and new immigrants.

It was the hand cattlemen had been waiting for.

Year after year, the rancher had gambled his whole herd on the unpredictable mood of the elements, playing close to the table. But when the spring of 1903 rolled around, he decided the cards were finally stacked in his favor and threw in everything he owned for the big win.

Even the banks felt the fever, advancing loans at 10 per cent, throwing up new branches, and sending out their managers to stalk the streets for customers.

The stock boom, which had begun with the Klondike gold rush in 1898, was well under way by 1903. Thousands of range-bred steers were trailed in across the Montana border; thin animals from the over-grazed, sheeped-out U.S. range.

Prices were on the upswing. Big American outfits were establishing ranches on the Canadian side of the border, bringing in huge herds to grow fat on free Canadian grass.

Money was easy — too easy. With pockets full, Alberta ranchers decided they could afford the big gamble of speculating on cheap, farm-bred yearlings from Quebec, Ontario and Manitoba.

Speculation on eastern yearlings spread like wildfire, and by May 19, 1903, trains loaded with thousands of them were on the rails west.

The ranchers were taking a terrible chance. Open-range cattlemen of that day provided feed only for bulls, weaning calves, and saddle horses — and there was absolutely no precedent for supposing the eastern cattle would be able to acclimatize themselves well enough to rustle for forage on the open prairie when winter set in.

Ranchers knew the score, but they were betting everything on the hope for a mild winter. None of them, in those hot first days of May, realized he might better be praying for a mild spring.

On May 19, from all parts of the short grass country, ranchers and round-up crews gathered along the CPR tracks, listening to the far-off whistles of train after train loaded with eastern yearlings.

Unknown to them, miles to the west, a 16-year-old boy named Henry Cavan was staring upward at a whirling cauldron of grey cloud sweeping in across the Rockies. The boy shivered, pulled his jacket around him, and started to run eastward to shout warning.

The storm, too fast for his legs, raced past to announce itself.

It started with rain that lashed the traffic jam of trains and turned stockyards into seas of mud. As hours went by, the temperature dropped steadily and the rain began to have the sting of ice.

By the 20th, the rain had turned to snow, a raging blizzard with the temperature at 10 above zero and dropping steadily.

Inside the packed stock cars, yearlings were trampling one another to death, or simply perishing from the severity of cold they had never experienced before.

Desperate train crews and ranchers were throwing animals from cars so that still more trains could move into place and unload.

When stockyards grew too full, the yearlings were driven out, bawling and stumbling, to fight for their lives on the open prairie. It was a fight most of them lost.

Like everyone else, young Henry Cavan worked 20 hours a day during the seven days the storm lasted. There was no way to brand any of the calves, he recalls, and he and the other cowhands ended up simply tying rag identifying bands around the animals' necks before driving them out into the storm.

The storm finally broke on the morning of May 27. But its effects — two-foot deep snow and drifts too high to ride a horse through — would linger until the end of June.

Unable to paw through to the grass under the snow, the yearlings continued to perish by the hundreds.

Grim-faced ranchers began the chilling task of counting their losses.

Dan Hamilton: 2,500 lost of 6,500 head. Spencer Bros. of Milk River: 1,200 lost of 5,000. Albert Desbrisay, Sage Creek: 500 lost of 1,000. Western Pack Company: 1,500 lost of 3,500.

And on it went. By the time the count was over, the short grass ranchers had lost 50 per cent of the eastern yearlings during the storm alone.

Desperately, ranchers tried to strengthen the survivors during the remaining weeks of summer. But winter came too soon and too hard, and outfit after outfit was wiped out completely.

Cresswell and Day, for example, had saved close to 4,000 of the 8,000 yearlings they had on the doomed trains — only to lose them all to the onset of winter.

It had been a great gamble, a great adventure — the last fling for the short grass rancher.

As one recalled defensively later: "Why, doggone it, a man couldn't associate with himself no more if he threw in a hand like that."

In the aftermath of empty range and 10-percent loans that would lead to foreclosure, rancher after rancher went out of business.

Those who were left, like young Henry Cavan, found themselves turning reluctantly to a new way of ranching: digging irrigation canals and becoming half farmers to grow winter feed.

They themselves finally put an end to open range, helping to string the barb wire ranchers have always hated.

Today, of course, those like Henry Cavan realize the changes were inevitable; the spring blizzard of 1903 only hastened the process.

And today they are the first to acknowledge that the results — in larger, better-managed ranches and more efficient handling of cattle — have given Alberta ranching a stability it would never have had otherwise.

But, sometimes, they can't help but wonder what would have happened if the biggest gamble in ranching history had somehow paid off . . .

SOD-BUSTING

"On our way back, we passed by Charlie's place and got treated to an astonishing sight. There was old Charlie at the plough, dressed in nothing but his underwear and boots and covered with dust from head to foot.

"As he passed us, urging his ox on with oats and a stick, I demanded: What are you doing out in nothing but your underwear, Charlie?

" 'Well,' he answered, not stopping, 'it makes more sense than getting my clothes dirty, doesn't it?'

"Unable to think of a suitable reply, we just sat and watched this unusual spectacle until the hour forced us to shake up the team and get on back to Diamond City."

* * * *

A FAIR GROWTH OF PLANTS & FLOWERS . . .

Most people today — even in Alberta — take the province's prominence in the field of agriculture pretty much for granted. It wasn't always so.

In 1859, at the request of the British government, Captain

John Palliser was exploring what is now southern Alberta. One purpose of the trip was to fill in blank spaces on the map of Canada.

But the main purpose was to report back on the resource and agricultural prospects in the unknown west.

Palliser's report on southern Alberta wasn't encouraging: "The whole region as far as the eye could reach was at times covered by buffalo in herds varying from hundreds to thousands. The grass was eaten off the earth as if the place had been devastated by locusts."

Describing the areas as unfit for agriculture, he sent in his report and a map that identified the treeless grassland as "arid plains".

Only a few years later, however, a botanist travelling through the same country sent a different report back east. It spoke of ample rainfall and of "a fair growth of plants and flowers".

What the botanist had encountered, of course, was only the freak of a wet year. But he and the people who read his report didn't know that.

By 1880, prospective homesteaders in eastern Canada and Europe were being urged to the Canadian west — a land where it took only the turn of a plough to uncover security and happiness — and thousands of sod-busters were eagerly pursuing the dream.

None of the newcomers knew about the Palliser report, of course, But it wasn't too long before those who turned the soil of southern Alberta found themselves writing "arid plains" on the bitter, personal map of experience.

It would take long years of struggle and the irrigation talents of the Mormon pioneers at Cardston to turn those arid plains into the "garden" of the prairies.

* * * *

AND APPLAUSE OF THE SPECTATORS . . .

The rush of homesteaders to Alberta, which started in 1880, continued almost unchecked until well past the First World War. Dazzled by the promotion efforts expended on them before they came west, most settlers were unprepared for the hardships of the land. And fewer still were prepared to handle the surprising amount of trouble it sometimes took just to get into the land office.

The following account, from the Lethbridge Herald of June 6, 1910, illustrates the point all too clearly:

"What is supposed to be an organized gang of 'bull-rushers', as they are known to the police, land office officials and others, received a setback this morning when they endeavored to turn the well known trick of ejecting by brute force the man holding first place at the land office in the rush for a homestead thrown open for settlement.

"This morning it was land situated near Grassy Lake that became open. It was previously owned as a pre-emption by William C. Llewelyn but he having recently sold his homestead, by the regulations the pre-emption automatically became vacant.

"Llewelyn, however, had the right to purchase a homestead and thus he was attempting to apply on this quarter this morning.

"According to a land office official, at half past eight there were only two or three men present, Llewelyn and one or two others, who had been there since Friday or Saturday.

"Two or three minutes before nine o'clock, however, a gang which had operated at numerous other rushes, drove up in a couple of automobiles and immediately made a set at Llewelyn and forced him and his friends away, taking possession of the steps.

"A number of spectators assembled and sided immediately with Llewelyn, with the result that a sort of Donnybrook fair scene was enacted. Someone ran for the police and Constable Taylor arrived and later Sergt. Lamb.

"They stopped the fighting but there their powers ceased.

"Agent Stafford, who had witnessed the whole affair, however, came out and asked them to eject off the premises the whole crowd with the exception of young Llewelyn.

"This action was taken amid the cheers and applause of the spectators."

This particular story ends happily. But there was many a newcomer — particularly among those who spoke no English — who fared far worse than the lucky Mr. Llewelyn.

* * * *

THE COURTSHIP OF VERA . . .

With so many hardships to overcome in wresting a living from the land, Alberta's early farmers had to depend heavily on enterprise and ingenuity.

This enterprise and ingenuity often paid off — even, as a young man named John Jackson discovered, in the romance department.

The young Mr. Jackson was unlucky enough to have a homestead right in the middle of Captain Palliser's dreaded triangle. But he was lucky enough to have a best girl named Vera, and he was determined to win her.

John was tireless in his courtship of Vera; more tireless it turned out than the battered buggy he used to make the long trips back and forth between her home and his.

Punished by the rutted trails, the buggy just plain gave out, one wheel threatening to come right off the hub.

With no new wheel available — and with no money to buy one even if it was — it looked for a few gloomy days like the end of a beautiful romance.

John, however, was in love, and he wasn't about to let some fool buggy stand in the way.

One afternoon a startled Vera rushed outside to find a grinning John driving up to the door in a squealing apparition.

On the hub where the ailing wheel had been, John's buggy now wore the bottom of a wooden tub.

John had come to ask an important question and, faced with so much determination, how could a girl say no?

The 'tub-buggy', incidentally, held together long enough to carry the blushing Vera 50 miles to Medicine Hat and back again to begin a happy new life as Mrs. John Jackson.

* * * *

WOOING THE DUST BOWL . . .

There were probably few places in the country in 1880 that could match southern Alberta as a frustrator of farmers.

At first glance, the area seemed to be a wonderland for homesteading. It was relatively easy to accumulate large parcels of land for virtually nothing. There were no trees to clear away and few rocks. And the soil itself was rich, sandy loam.

All that was missing was water. There wasn't enough rain, and what little there was didn't fall at the right time. It takes 30,000 gallons of water to raise a bushel of wheat, and 500,000 gallons to raise a ton of hay.

The homesteaders, whose large holdings earned them the title of Canada's wheat barons, tried anyway. Their ploughs ripped up the centuries-thick buffalo grass to expose the rich soil for planting — and trouble.

Although the homesteaders couldn't realize it, the buffalo grass was all that was holding southern Alberta down. By stripping away the grass, the homesteaders had simply turned the earth over to the prevailing west winds.

Dismayed homesteaders stood by helpless as wind erosion blasted great craters in the unprotected soil, tore loose precious seed, and created dust clouds that turned high noon as black as night.

Size was no protection. The late Charles Noble, after whom the village of Nobleford is named, was one of the biggest of the "wheat barons". He measured his holdings in townships, but went broke twice.

It was only his ingenuity that kept him from going broke a third time — and that gave the farmer one of his most valuable tools. Realizing his enemy was the wind, Noble invented a device called the Noble blade; a sub-soil tiller that leaves trash cover to hold down the surface of the soil.

The invention became world-famous, but even with it, Noble could count on no more than two or three good years in ten because of the lack of moisture.

Noble himself managed to struggle on. Most of his neighbors weren't able to.

As years went by, the concerned federal government and the CPR, which was bringing homesteaders west, realized that irrigation was the only answer if southern Alberta farm land was going to produce.

Fortunately, the irrigation expertise they needed was already in Alberta, in the small Mormon settlement at Cardston. The Mormons had raised irrigation techniques to a fine art during the long years in their old home of Utah, and they were using it to keep their Alberta holdings green.

Indeed, one of the first projects of the colony had been to dig irrigation ditches to tap the precious water of the St. Mary's River.

Industrialist C.A. Magrath (later to become mayor of Lethbridge) was one of the first to approach the Mormons. He offered Charles Ora Card 30,000 acres of land at a dollar an acre if the Mormons would dig an irrigation canal through it.

Card wouldn't commit his people to the $30,000 purchase, but the offer finally led to the Mormons undertaking to build the canal under contract.

Work started in August, 1898, and was finished two years later. Precious water was flowing from the St. Mary's River all along the Milk River Ridge toward Lethbridge. An extension of the irrigation canal brought water into the city itself.

Soon Mormon experts were being called to Ottawa to advise the federal government, and soon the CPR committed itself to the long, slow job of watering Palliser's dust bowl.

In 1935, the federal government stepped into the act directly with the formation of the Prairie Farm Rehabilitation Administration.

Today that irrigated area — only four percent of the province's worked land — produces twenty per cent of Alberta's agricultural output.

Through construction of the St. Mary's Dam, and the St. Mary–Milk Rivers projects, water is being tapped and fed into a system that irrigates more than a million acres of southern Alberta.

Where Charles Noble once struggled to survive, 7,500 irrigation farmers are now producing nearly $170 million in cereal and specialty crops and livestock.

It took more than a century, but the Alberta farmer has finally erased "Arid Plains" from Captain John Palliser's warning map.

* * * *

HOW SWEET IT IS . . .

Ever since a homesteader named Francis Willock found a few heads of Golden Chaff in his jacket pocket and planted them in the soil near Pincher Creek, Alberta has been known as wheat country.

Not without justification. Even in a modest crop year, enough Alberta wheat is harvested to feed 6 million people.

But wheat isn't the whole story of Alberta agriculture. Indeed, it wasn't even the beginning of farming here.

If legend is to be believed, farming in Alberta started with a fur-trader's liking for potatoes. Whether or not Peter Pond (one of the original partners in the North West Company) actually did start the whole thing in the 1700's with an addiction to spuds is impossible to prove.

But whoever started it, today more than half a billion dollars a year in field crops comes from the successors to Alberta's early kitchen gardens.

There are apples in Edmonton, strawberries at Morrin,

and red currants at Beaverlodge.

And from thousands of Alberta acres comes the sweet success of the sugar beet.

Driving the highway between Lethbridge and Medicine Hat in the fall, the motorist soon begins to think the whole world is filled with sugar beets. In field after field, farmers are pulling the brown-skinned vegetables. Every few miles, by the sides of the road, the motorist can see huge piles of millions of the beets.

And ahead and behind him roar big trucks loaded with still more beets. Beets bounce on the road, lie in the ditch — seem almost to fall from the sky.

It all started through a man named Jesse Knight founder of the town of Raymond), and as an off-shoot of the irrigation program in southern Alberta.

As the present century started, the first irrigation scheme was well underway. Men like Jesse Knight realized, from the start, that the only way to make the relatively small irrigated area turn a profit was to come up with some high-yield crop for which there was a ready market.

The sugar beet was a natural, and Jesse Knight had little trouble interesting C.A. Magrath, manager of the Canadian Northern and Alberta Railway and Irrigation Companies, in the scheme.

Magrath, in turn, soon had the federal government interested.

By 1902, Magrath and Knight had stirred up enough official interest to start a beet sugar factory at Raymond.

The factory wasn't built as a commercial enterprise so much as a service to the settlers of the area.

According to the contracts involved, the plant was to be kept in operation for 12 years.

But, right from the day it opened, the beet-sugar business

at Raymond was in trouble. The biggest problem was one that the planners hadn't foreseen — lack of interest by the farmers.

Oriented to wheat and livestock, and unfamiliar with the process of raising the beets, the farmer just stayed away.

Faced with a shortage of beets, Knight appealed to the federal government for assistance. The government, which looked on the plant as potent development force in the province, responded with a bonus scheme.

The bonus paid 50 cents a hundred pounds of sugar, the amount to be divided equally between farmer and plant.

And, to further bolster the operation, the government eliminated all taxes on the plant for the 12 years of the contract.

The action by the government was enough to keep the plant going for the 12 years of the contract, but it did little to overcome the problem of farmer disinterest. It would take a streak of bad luck to do that.

Shortly after the contract had ended, Knight and his associates closed the Raymond plant and moved the operation to Cornish, Utah, where the sugar beet was an established crop.

If the Alberta farmer didn't miss the plant right away, he did in a few short years. With the ending of the First World War, the grain farmer was hit by drought and falling prices.

Forced to find another crop, he rediscovered the sugar beet and was soon clamouring for a new sugar plant. But the clamour went unheard and farm after farm went under, abandoned to the weeds.

The CPR colonization office found itself with hundreds of parcels of land — many of them irrigated — turned back by discouraged or destitute owners.

In the small communities of Raymond and Magrath, the boards of trade set up a committee to try to persuade some beet processor to set up the desperately-needed plant in the area.

Soon the committee was concentrating on one company in particular, the Utah-Idaho Sugar Company, a firm which was already interested in entering southern Alberta with a factory.

It was 1922 before the negotiations paid off.

The sugar company, before agreeing to come to the area, demanded some specific evidence of good faith to make sure they didn't suffer the same fate as the earlier operation.

The primary conditions were that farmers would grow trial plots in all areas in 1923 so that yield could be measured; that 6,000 acres of good land would be summer-fallowed to company standards and irrigated in the summer of 1924; and that provisional contracts be signed to guarantee the growth of 6,000 acres of beets in 1925.

It took a great deal of scrambling, but the committee managed to meet the conditions, and by 1925 a new plant was going up at Raymond.

For miles around, farmers were turning the country into an enormous beet patch; meeting and overcoming all the inevitable problems involved in handling a new crop.

That first year, 1925, was the critical one if the industry was going to survive, and somehow the farmers made it — despite an almost-fatal last-minute blow from nature.

Early in August, with harvest approaching, the area was lashed by heavy rains that continued, with few respites, until the end of October. And, on Sept. 25, a storm piled 16 inches of snow on the beet fields, making harvesting almost impossible.

Somehow or other, the farmers managed to harvest anyway. They cleared 5,394 acres and poured almost 42,000 tons of beets into the new plant.

From that point on, despite occasional problems, there was no looking back. The Raymond plant has long since closed, but new companies are in operation at Picture Butte and Taber.

They stand today in lasting vindication of Jesse Knight, who history proved didn't have the wrong idea. Rather, he just had the right idea a little too early.

* * * *

ALBERTA'S MR. AGRICULTURE . . .

The changes in Alberta's agricultural industry in the past 60 years have been phenomenal — so phenomenal that the farmer's biggest complaint today is his ability to grow too much.

It's a complaint the early sod-busters would have been glad to make.

Mechanization has replaced the old scythe, rake and threshing flail with huge, rumbling combines that can do in minutes what once took days and weeks.

Perhaps more important than mechanization, however, are the radical improvements in growing-techniques themselves.

And that's where we come to the late Dr. William Fairfield. From 1901 on, whether he was inoculating an alfalfa field or urging his staff on in efforts to find new strains of wheat, Dr. Fairfield held the prime place in Alberta's agricultural revolution.

The Ontario-born agriculture expert first came to Alberta to operate a demonstration farm outside Lethbridge for the Canadian North-West Irrigation Company.

In August, 1906, the Canada department of agriculture decided to establish an experimental station at Lethbridge, and Bill Fairfield was chosen to run it.

Dr. Fairfield attracted attention in agriculture circles right from the day he arrived in Alberta.

A missionary for better farming, he preached his theories, then put them into practice so well that farmers all over the province were imitating him.

Soon Bill Fairfield was the man to see if you had a farm problem.

Even Mormon leader Charles Ora Card, something of a farming wizard himself, went to Fairfield for advice.

Card's problem was alfalfa; the foundation crop of irrigation farming. Although Card had been able to grow alfalfa in Utah, he just couldn't make it come up in Alberta. Already Card's colonists at Cardston had written off the area as "just not alfalfa country," but Card himself wasn't convinced.

Nor was the young Dr. Fairfield. Intrigued by the puzzle, he recalled he had read somewhere that alfalfa seed needs inoculation so that it can take nitrogen from the air. Maybe, he wondered, this could be the problem.

To test the theory, he sent to Wyoming for a bag of soil in which alfalfa had been successfully grown. When he sprinkled the soil over a spindly field, he delighted Card and astonished the whole countryside.

The alfalfa responded almost immediately, and grew a lush crop the next year. Soon his "inoculated" alfalfa was an important part of the farming scene. Indeed, Dr. Fairfield always maintained that it was the alfalfa discovery that was his most important contribution to Alberta agriculture.

It was only one contribution of hundreds, however. Under his careful supervision, a network of agriculture research stations was set up in the province, farmers were being taught vital lessons about erosion-prevention and fertilization.

Under Fairfield's guidance, researchers began producing new strains of plants specially suited to conditions in Alberta.

Marquis wheat, produced under his program in 1910, is still the standard by which wheat quality is measured.

Strains resistant to sawfly — Rescue, Chinook and Cypress — followed. Chinook, in particular, has won the World Wheat King title for several Alberta farmers.

The list goes on and on: Galt and Betze barley, Winalta winter wheat, Beaver alfalfa, Chinook potato . . .

All Alberta today is a living, growing tribute to the work he started and carried through.

But perhaps nothing pays better tribute to Dr. William Fairfield than the trees he urged on southern Alberta.

When he arrived, the prairie was bare. Today thousands of trees stand as his monument, and as the symbols of the Alberta farmer's hard-won victory over a demanding new land.

EARLY SETTLEMENT

BONNET FOR A CHIEF . . .

Although his audience was only a few white men, Thunder Bird, the mighty Cree chief, told his story with care and skill:

"Twenty-one winters ago Red Deer, a chief of the Crees, was camped with his tribe where the river that bears his name joins the swift flowing water.

"In one of his teepees lived a beautiful maiden that I loved, Silver Rose by name. Her voice was soft and sweet as the brook rippling over the sun-kissed pebbles and her eyes when she smiled shone with a love that would endure as long as the stars kept watch.

"Red Deer, although he already had four squaws, forced her against her will to marry him and live in his teepee. When I heard of this I rode with two of my swiftest cayuses to his camp and eloped with her. We fled to the great bend in the river where it runs nearest to the Cypress Hills.

"The action caused Red Deer and his braves to go on the warpath and, for a time, civil war threatened among the Crees.

"Silver Rose, however, knowing of Red Deer's love of display and showy feathers, sent me to shoot a number of eagles nesting on the high cut-banks along the river.

"From seven of the best-matched of these, she selected the finest tail feathers and wrought them into one of the most beautiful bonnets any chief ever possessed.

"When this bonnet was presented to Red Deer as a peace offering it caused such a remarkable change in him that our people, being very superstitious, attributed the change to magic or medicine possessed by the bonnet or hat, hence it became known as The Saamis. Consequently the place where the hat was made became known as the place of The Saamis — the Medicine Hat."

The chief, his story finished, waited in expectant silence. One of the white men stirred and, clearing his throat, leaned forward.

"That hat," he told Thunder Bird, "must have possessed wonderful medicine to appease the wrath of the irate chief. I, therefore, shall in honor of your noble squaw who has played such an important part in these events name the place Medicine Hat."

The speaker was Sir William Van Horne of the Canadian Pacific Railway. And, as anyone visiting southeastern Alberta today knows, he kept his promise to Thunder Bird.

* * * *

WHERE THERE'S SMOKE . . .

Further north, other white men were listening to another Indian story that would give birth to a modern Alberta community, the community of Wetaskiwin.

The story is set more than a hundred years ago, when the Cree and Blackfoot were still fighting, raiding north

and south across the Red Deer River that separated their
territories.

A party of Blackfoot had pushed north across the river,
following the buffalo on their summer migration — and
taking the opportunity to raid Cree camps for ponies and
scalps.

The Blackfoot party, late in the summer, were camped
on the banks of Pipestone Creek. The Cree were out for
blood and had rushed a large force south to cut off the re-
treat of their enemies.

All day the Blackfoot sat in council of war, listening
to the muffled drums of the Cree.

If the Blackfoot were worried by their position, there
was nothing in their council of war to show it. Far from
mapping out escape plans, they were hatching a scheme
to raid the Cree camp by night and return home with even
more horses and scalps.

It just wasn't Blackfoot nature to avoid a fight.

At that time, each of the tribes had a powerful young
chief rising to leadership: Little Bear for the Cree and
Buffalo Child for the Blackfoot.

When the Blackfoot were ready to scout the Cree camp
to make the raid, it was Buffalo Child who was sent on the
mission. By coincidence, the Cree were in the process of
doing some scouting of their own, and Little Bear was
doing it.

Being talented scouts, both men wanted to find the best
vantage point from which to spy on the enemy's camp. Only,
as it turned out, the best vantage point for both sides happened to be the same hill.

The two young chiefs stole up opposite sides of the hill
at the same time and, with a shock, suddenly found themselves face to face.

The two froze in their tracks, recognizing one another instantly. For a full minute they glared at one another, then Buffalo Child threw aside his rifle with a scornful smile.

"Dog of a Cree," he taunted. "See, I throw my gun away. I do not need it. With my bare hands I will break you in two."

With equal scorn, Little Bear tossed his knife aside. "No Blackfoot with the heart of a woman can get the better of Little Bear."

They circled warily, looking for an opening, spitting insults at each other. Then, like two great cats, they sprang and grappled.

The two were almost a match for size and strength and neither could gain an advantage. Locked in one another's grasp, they swayed and struggled. First the Cree would go down, then the Blackfoot, but neither for long enough to give his enemy victory.

For almost an hour, as the sun slowly set, the two struggled on in silence. Then, as though by mutual consent, they drew apart, panting, and exhausted.

"You are a stout fighter," the Blackfoot admitted as he gasped for air. "Let us rest awhile and, later, we will renew the struggle."

Little Bear grunted agreement, and the two squatted, facing one another. The fierce hatred in their eyes was now mixed with something almost like respect.

Buffalo Child fumbled at his belt and pulled forth a pipe and tobacco from a beaded bag. Little Bear followed his example, but found his pipe had been broken into three pieces during the fight.

Frustrated, he threw the clay fragments aside, then sat back enviously to watch his enemy smoke.

Slowly, the Blackfoot filled his pipe, lighted it, and began to puff complacently.

The sweet smell of 'kinnikinic' smoke almost drove Little Bear wild. He smouldered with rage at his enemy's enjoyment of a pleasure that was denied him.

All this was not lost on Buffalo Child. It was a form of torture which an Indian could appreciate. He watched Little Bear with amusement. Suddenly, perhaps to heighten the torture, he held the smoking pipe out to his Cree opponent.

Before he could pull back his hand, Little Bear had snatched the pipe free, thrust the mouthpiece between his lips, and inhaled deeply.

Abruptly, he stopped with a strangled cough and stared at Buffalo Child. Buffalo Child, equally aghast, was staring back, mouth open with consternation.

An incredible thing had been done. Impulsively, through an act of fate, they had accidentally smoked together the common pipe.

It was the sacred pledge of amity and peace, made so by immemorial tradition, as unbreakable to them as the most solemn vow.

Finally, the Cree spoke. "My brother," he said softly, "we did not mean to do it, but we have smoked the peace pipe together. Henceforth we must be friends, and because we are chiefs of our tribes, our people also must be friends and think no more of war. Is it not so?"

Reluctantly, Buffalo Child agreed. He rose to his feet. "We must go back to the lodges of our people," he said, "and tell them of this thing we have done." He shivered in the growing darkness.

"I cannot understand it, but some great medicine must have been at work. Undoubtedly it is a sign; it must be the will of the Manitou. Let us go."

They turned on their heels, two dejected and bedraggled

figures, and silently parted in the dusk.

The following morning, runners were sent from the camp of the Crees to summon the Blackfoot to council. During the night, on both sides, the older chiefs had listened gravely to the incredible story and shaken their heads in puzzlement. But all admitted that what had been done could not be undone.

Tradition could not be overridden lightly. And, without a doubt, it must be a sign from the Great Manitou.

In early morning, the council assembled on the hilltop where the struggle had taken place. Four chiefs of the Blackfoot and six of the Cree sat in solemn circle and passed the pipe of peace from hand to hand.

There were pledges of eternal friendship and peace, and the hatchet was buried with appropriate ceremony.

Ever since, outwardly at least, Cree and Blackfoot have respected the vows they exchanged.

And ever since, the hills outside one of Alberta's bustling communities have been known as "Weteskewin Spatinow" — the place where peace was made.

*   *   *   *

"People are gregarious and life is too short to spend years in isolation" — Sen. F. W. Gershaw

LET US GATHER TOGETHER . . .

At first, the Alberta pioneer called the isolation of the praire "freedom", and revelled in it.

But soon he was calling it "loneliness", and he was suffering from it.

It was no accident that those who had known pioneer life before — like the Mormon settlers at Cardston — built their community outward from the nucleus of a town.

They knew that illness and injury were risks too high to run alone, and silence too great a burden to bear in isolation.

Certainly most Alberta towns and villages began for economic reasons; as centres of transportation or trade. But what made all of them grow was a pressing need for community. The rest came naturally.

* * * *

AT THE MOUTH OF THE ELBOW . . .

Rev. John McDougall, who had seen Edmonton change from trading post to town, who had seen Whoop-up go up and come down, was in southern Alberta in the summer of 1875 in time to witness the birth of what would be Alberta's giant city of the south.

Reading his journal of the events of that summer and fall when he was clearing land to raise a home and a mission, one can't help but wonder if he didn't have a slight premonition of things to come . . .

"It was sometime in September that I was putting on the first shingled roof in Alberta south of Edmonton when some Indians reported that a company of white men were at the mouth of the Elbow River and acted as if they were going to build and winter there.

"What did I know about it? I told them I did not know that such was the case but that I would soon find out.

"As I thought over this report, I remembered having very strongly commended this very spot to Col. Macleod as a suitable centre for a police detachment. I had pointed out that it was on the direct line from Fort Macleod to Edmonton House, also that there were at that time several frequented passes across the mountains by way of the Bow and Kananaskis rivers. In addition, all the balance of the country was easily accessible from this point, thus it was from every viewpoint strategic. So I thought it possible Colonel Macleod might be acting on my suggestion. Therefore I determined to know as soon as possible.

"Immediately after dinner I changed my clothes, saddled my horse and galloped down the valley of the Bow, and in the waning of the day came into sight of the mouth of the Elbow.

"Here, sure enough, was an encampment of a company of Mounted Police. As it was near dark I did not want to make the ford that night. Looking around I saw a solitary lodge on the flat on the north side of the river.

"Riding over to this I found it belonged to an old acquaintance of mine, a French mixed breed of whom I spoke in the volume preceding this as the man who smuggled whiskey into our fort on the hill in 1873-4. He and his wife welcomed me to their lodge.

"I noticed that they were somewhat embarrassed in so doing and while I was tethering my horse I saw disappearing over the hill a man who doubtless had crawled out the rear of the lodge as I came to the front.

"Then I recollected it was one of the sons of this man who had stolen my horse the season before and now I was sure this was the thief who was running away.

"While the man and woman were preparing some supper and making me comfortable I told the father to go out to the hill and signal to his son to come in and to assure him that I did not intend to lay any charge against him, indeed I had absolutely forgiven him the theft.

"This the father gladly went and did and before my supper was ready brought in the young man and presented him to me as the boy who had brought shame upon his people by stealing the horse from such a person as I was. I gave the young fellow some advice and cautioned him as to the future.

"After an early breakfast I forded the Bow and presently was welcomed into the camp by the police. Here I soon learned that my surmise was correct.

"This spot had been selected and here was a full company of police for the building of a fort. Already up on the Elbow was a gang of men under Mr. Davis, one of my quondam friends of the Whoop-up scenes, taking out timber for this purpose. The contract for the building had been given to the I.G. Baker & Co. of Fort Benton.

"Captain Brisbois, the commanding officer and myself, rode up the Elbow that same morning and dined with Mr. Davis and his men at their timber camp.

"That night I slept in one of the officer's tents and the next day rode back to Morley and told the Indians what was being done.

"Some were quite indignant that another post was being placed, as they said, right in the path of the buffalo. This would entail hunger and possibly starvation to the Indians. In addition, what right had the white man at this time to establish centres without the government conferring first about it with the Indians?

"I explained, apologized and sought to give them assurance. At the same time I told them that the days of the buffalo were being numbered, that no earthly power could stay the change that was coming.

"I reminded them that both my father and myself had told them the truth about these changes ever since we had come into the western country. I concluded by stating that the presence of this post at the mouth of the Elbow would be the best guarantee of peace, both with Indians and white men, we could have.

"Many of the head men acquiesced in this but a number were sullen and disgruntled because of this new move. We had therefore to intensify our efforts along the lines of conciliation and education. Many a prolonged night council I held at that time and for years afterwards.

". . . Immediately following our making known the fact that the police were establishing themselves at the Elbow, the Hudson's Bay post master moved down there from Ghost River and commenced to build beside them. I.G. Baker and Company also started to build in the vicinity.

"Thus in a few weeks the mouth of the Elbow became a busy scene of government occupancy and trade development . . ."

That "busy scene of government occupancy and trade development", of course, was the beginning of Fort Calgary.

The old fort has long since gone, but a few years ago it provided a rare glimpse at how close Alberta's past really is to the present.

A team from the University of Calgary was digging in the downtown area in a bid to find the foundations of the old fort. As they dug, they attracted many spectators — including a handful of old-timers who kept insisting they were digging in the wrong place, and who urged them to try another spot they described.

The university team, of course, had worked out its calculations well and were sure they were in the right place and weren't about to take advice from sidewalk engineers.

When, months later, the team had to abandon the search site, someone remembered the advice of the old-timers and the team decided to give it a try.

At the new dig, right where the old-timers had said, was the foundation of the fort.

ON MY BACK PORCH

ON MY BACK PORCH ...

" ... for the new settlers in their humble homes inconveniences did everywhere abound. It was the day of the tallow candle and the coal-oil lamp. It was the day of slab and tar-paper shacks.

"Mail was something one did not expect until it arrived. There was no certainty nor regularity in its delivery, whether by stage-coach or by train.

"All these things were part of the heavy curtain of silence and far distance that cut off the adventurous souls who had come from their dear ones left behind in other lands.

"Then, too, the uncertainties of a rigorous climate made it impossible for a traveller to know whether his journey would take him days or weeks. Because of the scarcity of stopping-places along the way there was a real danger in the matter of blizzards while on the trail. So travellers, except in the warmest season, usually were muffled to the ears in warm clothing ...

"Over against this, what do I see today?

"A man slips on a light coat or sweater over his suit,

puts on light rubbers (or maybe none at all) and jumps into a warm luxurious car or on a plane. In a matter of hours or even minutes he has reached his destination, be it a hundred miles or a thousand.

"Besides the daily mail he has hourly broadcasts of the world and home news by radio and TV.

"On my automatic dial telephone I talk to my daughter in Montreal in a matter of seconds. All, rich or poor, have electric lights in their homes, and many running water. Gone is the day when we depend on wood and coal for our fuel, with abundant supplies of fuel oil, propane and natural gas available.

"If I ride by night in the country districts, I find the whole scene lit up through the wonders of rural electrification. The neon lights of the small village on the west spread their beams to encircle my home grounds.

"I no longer look out on a dark wide world when I step on my back porch."

* * * *

There are hundreds of Albertans who, like pioneer writer Evangeline Warren, remember an Alberta far different from the one in which we live today.

They came to an untouched land. To the east and south it was a grassy plain slashed with coulees and cutbanks — the home of the buffalo. In its centre lay the badlands. To the west, forming an unpenetrated wall, were the mountains. To the north, it was forest and desert and a tangle of wild rivers plunging to the arctic.

Today, the buffalo are gone and the plains are a quilt of grain fields and grazing land. The mountains are safely tied down with ropes of rail and road.

The north, slowly, is giving up its secrets and its riches.

Even the badlands turned out to be not so bad after all.

And Evangeline Warren, in the introduction to her book "Seventy South Alberta Years," spoke of the trucks that now wakened her in the nights . . .